FLOWERING POT PLANTS

All Year Round

FLOWERING POT PLANTS
All Year Round

Gordon Procter

BLANDFORD PRESS
POOLE · DORSET

First published in the U.K. 1986 by Blandford Press,
Link House, West Street, Poole, Dorset, BH15 1LL.

Distributed in the United States by
Sterling Publishing Co., Inc.,
2 Park Avenue, New York, N.Y. 10016.

British Library Cataloguing in Publication Data

Procter, Gordon
  Flowering pot plants all year round
  1. Plants, Potted   2. Flower gardening
  I. Title
  635.9'65   SB418

ISBN 0 7137 1596 0

Typeset by Megaron Typesetting, Bournemouth

Printed in Yugoslavia

CONTENTS

Camellia japonica 'Mrs Tingley'.

PREFACE

Many books have been written on the subject of greenhouse gardening. Invariably they consist of two sections; the first deals with types of greenhouses, methods of heating and ventilation etc., and general greenhouse management; and the second consists of a comprehensive list of greenhouse plants, with usually a brief description of the plants, their culture and sometimes details of varieties.

Such books, and hundreds have been written during the past 200 years, are invaluable to the established greenhouse gardener, particularly as works of reference, but to the new greenhouse owner the long list of plants, most of which will be new to him, must be rather overwhelming. The purpose of this present work is to provide the newcomer with guidance, and at the same time to show how a greenhouse can be usefully employed the whole year round without the cost being beyond the owner's purse.

The foliage house plant is now a regular feature of our homes, but it does not replace a vase of flowers. Only a flowering pot plant can do this. If it is a question of buying either a flowering pot plant or a bunch of cut flowers, it is, in the long term, more economical to buy the pot plant if you know how to look after it.

The cost of heating your greenhouse is offset by the saving made in not having to buy flowers or plants once you have established your greenhouse collection which can provide the house with flowering pot plants throughout the whole year.

There are literally thousands of greenhouses in gardens which are completely unused during the late autumn and winter months. This seems such a waste when, for a modest outlay, the owners could utilise their greenhouses so usefully and profitably.

You could, for instance, house a collection of evergreen azaleas in pots, and the only time it would be necessary to provide any heat would be when the outside temperature falls below freezing point. A small paraffin stove would suffice and you would not burn many gallons of oil during the average winter. This would not interfere with the summer use of the greenhouse, because the azaleas are grown outside during this period.

Because the object of this book is to list a collection of plants and not a large and wide variety of all types of greenhouse plants, it is possible to give considerably more details about the origin, history and cultivation than you would find in the more general greenhouse publication.

It is, of course, appreciated that people have different tastes and one grower's collection could very well contain a number of plants which have no appeal to another grower. In the course of developing my present collection I have grown and discarded many different genera for one reason or another and no doubt I shall continue to do so as time goes by.

It is however necessary to grow a plant first, as well as your skill permits, and then, if it appeals to you, try its suitability under house conditions before you can decide whether it should be included in your collection. If you grow every plant described in this book in this way, you will, at the very least, fill your house with flowers, and then you can develop your own tastes by discarding and replacing the genera of plants which do not appeal to you.

G.P. 1984

Gloxinias and fuchsias in the greenhouse.

THE GREENHOUSE

The function of the greenhouse is to provide the ideal environment for the plants growing in it, but as this is hardly possible when many different kinds of plants are being grown, the object should be to strive to create the most favourable conditions for the main types of plants which are being housed at any particular time. A greenhouse which is large enough to divide into two compartments increases the scope of the grower, particularly in the colder months of the year, because one compartment can be used for cool greenhouse plants at a minimum temperature of 45°F (7°C), and the other kept just frost-proof for hardier plants.

The modern greenhouse is all glass, allowing maximum light, usually with an aluminium frame, which requires no maintenance, and will last the owner's lifetime.

There are two points worth bearing in mind when choosing and erecting an aluminium greenhouse. A sliding door is preferable to an opening door because there is less likelihood of damage by the wind; also it can be left partially open on hot days in the summer to improve the ventilation. Medium size glass panes are much easier to replace in case of breakage than the very large panes which are a feature of some makes, and you will inevitably experience broken panes in the course of time.

When erecting a metal greenhouse it is most important to ensure that it stands on a firm base, so that there is no possibility of subsidence. Glass is a heavy material and there is considerable weight in a greenhouse, so a solid concrete foundation is a necessity if future trouble is to be avoided. This is a very important point because should subsidence occur it would cause the metal framework of the greenhouse to develop a twist. When this happens it puts a strain on the glass, particularly at the spot where the glass-holding clip presses against the glass. Every time a gale occurs you would be very likely to find one or two cracked panes. Having personally experienced this fault in construction I can tell you with feeling that it is to be avoided if you wish to enter your greenhouse without a sinking feeling after every windy night.

One of the main advantages of glass-to-the-ground greenhouses is that you can grow plants in the beds, and pot plants can also be grown under the benches when room is in demand, which, with most enthusiasts, occurs every spring.

It is an advantage to have movable benches so that the whole greenhouse can be benched in the winter, and in the summer one or more benches can be moved out to utilise a bed for growing tomatoes or any other plants which require the full height of the greenhouse.

Having built your greenhouse, or acquired it from a previous owner, it is now necessary to consider the equipment required to produce the most favourable conditions for your plants.

As many people go out to work this means that, after popping into the greenhouse first thing in the morning, it is then left all day until you return home in the evening. Now this is hardly fulfilling the requirement of creating the most ideal environment for your plants, particularly in the spring and the autumn when the weather can change so rapidly.

Consider what can happen on a day in spring. You get up in the morning to a dull grey sky, the air is cold about 45°F (7°C), so you decide to leave all ventilating lights closed, and quite rightly, but by mid-morning the sky clears, the sun shines strongly and the temperature in your fully-closed greenhouse rises to over 100°F (37°C) and the plants do not like it. Neither do you when you see all the plants in the smaller pots drooping through lack of water.

Fortunately, nowadays, we are well provided with greenhouse aids and have a choice of systems for automatic heating, watering and ventilating.

AUTOMATIC VENTILATION

Automatic ventilators are a must for greenhouses which are left unattended all day, and there are various makes available which are easily fitted.

AUTOMATIC WATERING

Unless you wish to be involved in the daily chore, and on sunny days the twice-daily chore of hand watering all your plants, which can be very time consuming if you have a full greenhouse, you would be very well advised to install an automatic watering system. The initial cost of this can be quite high but the advantage of having a satisfactory system is invaluable, not only from the saving in labour, but from the point of view of providing the most favourable conditions for the plants.

One of the best watering systems works on the principle of capillary attraction and consists of a tray which is filled with sand or any inert powder which is capable of holding and conducting water. The sand is kept moist all the time and the pots are pressed on to the surface so that the moist sand is in direct contact with the compost in the pots. When plastic pots are used there is a sufficient number of drainage holes at the bottom of the pots to make adequate contact with the sand, but if clay pots are used, which have only one drainage hole, it is necessary to use a plug of fibreglass wool in the hole.

This method ensures an adequate supply of water for the plant because the water is being constantly replaced as it is being used. Moreover there is continuous evaporation of water from the surface of the moist sand between the pots; thus the plants are surrounded by a moist atmosphere even on hot sunny days.

In using these watering trays it is of course essential that the sand is not wet with excess water, and to avoid this it is necessary to control the height of the water feeding the sand. There are various different methods of doing this, one of which is a type of valve which is secured at the side of the tray and fed from a tank placed at a suitable height above the tray. This valve can be adjusted to alter the height of the water level under the surface of the sand. It is relatively inexpensive and enables the do-it-yourself man to make his own watering trays which can easily be constructed of wood, lined with heavy gauge polythene.

In recent times there has been a new development of this type of watering system with the introduction of capillary matting. This is an absorbent material which is simply laid on top of an ordinary greenhouse bench. When it is soaked with water it acts in the same way as a watering tray.

Obviously it is not as labour-saving because it will need soaking pretty frequently in hot weather, but it does have the advantage of being inexpensive and is certainly a much better method than hand watering.

It is, of course, possible to reduce the frequency of soaking the matting by placing a large bowl of water at the end of the matting, with a strip of matting connecting the water in the bowl to the capillary matting on the bench. The water in the bowl will flow by capillary action from the bowl to the bench matting and keep it moist as long as there is water in the bowl.

When a plant is grown on watering trays the compost in the pot is very moist and the pot feels much heavier than when it is watered by hand. It does, in fact, appear to be overwatered, but despite this I have yet to find a plant which does not thrive when watered by a watering tray.

AUTOMATIC HEATING

The heating systems used for greenhouses are usually electric, oil or gas powered, and so much literature is available that there is no need to give a detailed description here of the different methods. Whichever type of heating unit you decide to install, it is essential that it is adequate to raise the temperature of the greenhouse at least 20°F (11°C) above the ambient temperature. There are few nights in the average winter when the temperature drops to 10°F (5°C) below freezing point and a lift of 20°F (11°C) would give you a minimum temperature of 40 to 45°F (5 to 7°C).

Whichever system you choose it is highly desirable that you are able to control the temperature by thermostatic means, not just for the sake of ensuring that your plants are kept at the right temperature, but also for the sake of economy. All forms of heat are expensive these days, and there is no point in wasting it.

PROPAGATORS

As already mentioned it is a considerable advantage to divide your greenhouse into two compartments and during the winter months to endeavour to maintain an average temperature of 45°F (7°C) in one compartment. Although this temperature is sufficient to keep many mature plants growing, it is insufficient for the germination of seeds, the rooting of cuttings or for starting dormant tubers into growth. Most of these operations are carried out in late winter and spring, and as it is far too expensive to raise the temperature of the greenhouse a propagator is used.

It is invaluable to have a large propagator which will serve as a small greenhouse inside the larger one, because this increases your scope very considerably. It can be used not only for propagation but also for forcing plants, such as azaleas, into bloom whenever they are required, particularly when combined with artificial lighting. You should aim, therefore, to have a propagator which will fulfil all your requirements.

A home-made propagator will prove the most suitable in the long run and costs considerably less than proprietary models, which are not really large enough. Ideally it should be about 5–6 ft (1.5–1.8 m) in length, by 2½ ft (75 cm) in width, with 2½ ft (75 cm) headroom. A propagator this size with glass sides and top requires a 240-watt electric tubular heater with thermostatic control. If this propagator is housed in the cool compartment of the greenhouse it can be kept at a temperature of 60–70°F (15–21°C) for a low cost in the winter months.

ARTIFICIAL LIGHTING

Plant growth depends on a number of factors, two of which are light and heat. In the simplest of terms, plants convert water and carbon dioxide into complex carbohydrates. In order to enable the plant to carry out this synthesis it has to be supplied with energy. The plant absorbs light through its leaves every day, and by a process known as photosynthesis converts it into energy.

As some of the processes which take place in the plant are heat-sensitive, the ambient temperature is also a factor in the plant's growth.

It can easily be seen, therefore, that for optimum conditions for growth, a plant needs both heat and light in sufficient intensities. During the summer months these conditions are fulfilled naturally, but in the winter there is both insufficient heat and light.

During the period six weeks before and six weeks after the shortest day (the winter solstice) there are many days when the light intensity is insufficient to provide the plant with the energy required for the chemical synthesis to proceed, and consequently growth ceases.

It is therefore necessary to provide artificial light, as well as heat, during this period, if you wish to keep your plants growing.

All plants benefit when daylight is augmented by suitable artificial light at times when the light intensity is below average. If plants are given extra illumination on the numerous dull days the increase in growth will be considerable.

To use artificial light indiscriminately is merely incurring an unnecessary expense, but there are occasions when the benefits achieved are more than worth the cost. An illustration of this is in the growing of a cyclamen from a corm. After flowering, a cyclamen is rested by withholding water, which causes the corm to become dormant. It is usual to re-start the corm into growth in early summer, and if it is given a minimum temperature of 55°F (13°C) it will usually flower early in the winter. Few amateur gardeners can afford to provide such a high temperature in their greenhouses, but the same result can be achieved by providing a minimum temperature of 45°F (7°C) and artificial illumination for about ten hours a day during late autumn and early winter. They will remain in flower until late spring, if kept in a cool atmosphere without any further artificial light. If grown at 45°F (7°C) without any artificial light cyclamen will not usually flower before early spring.

Should you wish to use artificial light for any purpose other than augmenting daylight, it is necessary to ascertain the plant's light requirements, because plants vary in their requirements and the wrong application of artificial light might prove harmful. There are three main types of plants, as follows.

1. Short-day plants.
2. Long-day plants.
3. Day-neutral plants.

An example of a short-day plant is the chrysanthemum, which flowers in the autumn and winter. Until the days shorten to a certain number of hours, the flower buds do not form. By keeping a chrysanthemum in complete darkness for 14 hours in each 24 during the lighter months of the year, it can be induced to initiate flower buds and come into flower at any time of the year. In contrast, by exposing it to daylight plus artificial light for 14 hours a day it would never form any flower buds;

thus you can appreciate that it is necessary to know a plant's light requirements before extending the daylight period.

Some plants, such as the tomato plant, are day-neutral which means that they are not affected one way or the other by the length of time they are exposed to light, from the point of view of flower bud formation. They do, of course, benefit from being given extra light.

Long-day plants are plants which will not initiate flower buds until the day is beyond a critical length. Examples of this are certain varieties of fuchsia which will only form buds when the days are longer than 12 hours.

No doubt in future years all gardening books will include this kind of information in the same way as they give the plant's heat requirements.

To use artificial lighting it is not necessary to know all the technical terms, but merely to appreciate that the quality and the quantity of the light is important. As to the quality, the best source of light for the amateur gardener is the fluorescent tube. Of the different types available, the 'warm white' is the most suitable for general purposes if you are only using one tube; but a mixture of light, from one 'warm white' and one 'daylight', gives the best illumination if you have a two-tube fixture.

The quantity of light is governed by the length of time the plants are exposed to the artificial light and how close the fluorescent light tubes are positioned above the plants.

For use with the propagator already described, which is approximately 5½ ft (1.7 m) in length by 2½ ft (75 cm) in width, a unit consisting of two 5 ft (1.6 m) (80 watts each tube) fluorescent tubes is ideal, and units of this type are specially made for greenhouse use. The lighting unit should be suspended from the roof of the greenhouse in such a way that it can be lowered to within 2−3 in (5−7 cm) of the glass top of the propagator when in use, and when not in use can be secured close to the roof, out of the way and not casting a shadow on the propagator. It should be positioned centrally over the propagator to ensure that the light falls evenly over the whole area.

The intensity recommended for supplementary light is 10−18 watts per square foot (930 cm^2). The intensity is measured by dividing the wattage of the source of light by the area covered.

It will be obvious that, when artificial lighting is used, this necessitates switching the lights on and off at the correct times, and although this can be done by hand reasonably satisfactorily it is much more convenient and more flexible to incorporate a time switch in the lighting circuit, in the form of a clock which can be set to the precise times at which you require the lights to function. You will find it well worth the extra expense incurred in fitting an automatic time switch.

The advantage of using artificial light is well established and it is widely used by commercial growers. No doubt more and more amateur enthusiasts will make use of it as time goes on.

COMPOSTS

Much has been written about composts for pot plants and few gardeners will not have heard of the John Innes sowing and potting composts, which are widely offered wherever gardening requirements are sold. These composts are so called because they were developed as the result of several years' work at the John Innes Institute. Prior to that time there was no such thing as a standard potting compost and each gardener had his own formulae, and in most instances used different mixes for different plants.

As the result of the experiments carried out by the John Innes Institute it was shown that it is quite unnecessary, for the most part, to make up different composts for different plants.

The standard composts put forward by the JI Institute consist of one seed and cutting compost and three potting composts. The latter are known as John Innes potting composts Nos.1, 2 and 3. The difference between the three lies in the quantity of chemicals in the mix, and these chemicals are known as the John Innes base. No.2 contains twice as much as No.1, and No.3 three times as much. This provides the grower with three different strengths of potting compost. In addition to the John Innes base, a quantity of powdered chalk is added to the mix, except when preparing compost for plants which require an acid soil, such as heaths and rhododendrons, when it is omitted.

Apart from the chemicals and chalk, which are measured by weight, all the other ingredients of the compost, the loam (soil), peat and sand, are always measured by volume. This is important because, if measured by weight, the quantity would vary according to the water content, particularly in the case of the sand, and this would give rise to lack of uniformity.

A convenient method of measuring by volume is to use a standard seed tray which measures 14 × 8½ × 2 in (36 × 26 × 5 cm) and, for all practical purposes, nine such standard seed trays have a volume of approximately 1 bushel (8 gallons or 36 litres).

JI seed compost
2 parts fibrous loam.
1 part peat.
1 part washed sand.

To each bushel of the above mix add 1½ oz (42 g) superphosphate of lime and 1 oz (28 g) powdered chalk.

JI potting compost No.1
7 parts fibrous loam.
3 parts peat.
2 parts washed sand.

To each bushel of the above mix, add 4 oz (113 g) John Innes base and ¾ oz (21 g) powdered chalk.

The quantities of chemicals and chalk to add to make Nos.2 and 3 are as follows. For No.2 add 8 oz (227 g) John Innes base and 1½ oz (42 g) powdered chalk per bushel. For No.3 add 12 oz (340 g) John Innes base and 2¼ oz (64 g) powdered chalk per bushel. The fibrous loam most suitable for these composts is turves which have been stacked and allowed to stand for some six to nine months. If this is not available you can use topsoil from a plot which has been kept rich in humus by the addition of garden compost from year to year.

The loam used in making any of these composts should always be sieved through a ⅜-in (1-cm) riddle. The peat should be one of the fine grades, the sand should be a washed or horticultural grade, not builder's sand, and preferably a coarse sand.

The method I use when making composts is first of all to measure out the loam and put it in a heap. On top of this I put the measured quantity of peat followed by the sand. Before adding the sand to the heap, the JI base and any other chemicals, but not the chalk, are mixed with the sand. This helps to spread the chemicals throughout the mix. Using a spade the

heap is turned over a few times and then the powdered chalk is sprinkled over the heap as evenly as possible, after which the heap is turned over until all the ingredients are thoroughly mixed. The compost is then stored in a plastic bag of the type used for packing peat. Usually the loam, peat and sand contain sufficient moisture to be in the ideal state for use, i.e. if a handful is squeezed it just holds together, neither falling apart nor congealing into a solid lump. If the ingredients are too dry it is as well to add sufficient water, using a watering can with a rose, to correct this.

You can if you wish make up your own John Innes base according to the following formula.

By weight:
3 parts hoof and horn meal.
3 parts superphosphate of lime.
1½ parts sulphate of potash.

The main difference between JI composts and the composts of yesteryear is that the soil is sterilised by heating it to a minimum temperature of 180°F (82°C), the object being to destroy weed seeds, fungus and insects which may be present. The JI composts you buy have been treated in this way, but if you decide to make your own composts you will need to obtain a steriliser, if you consider it important to sterilise the soil. Personally I do not consider it necessary to sterilise the soil you use in a compost (neither did the very successful Victorian gardeners) unless there is reason to suppose it is infected in some way, in which case it should not be used.

In my very long experience of plant culture I have never suffered any deleterious effects from using unsterilised loam, and I have always made my own composts; but then gardening is, of course, like this. Some people do all the things which the text books say you should not do, and get excellent results, so it is not wise to be dogmatic when dealing with nature.

Most enthusiastic greenhouse gardeners are keen to fill their greenhouses, and this inevitably means the use of considerable quantities of potting compost; so it is really essential to mix your own composts from the point of view of the expense involved.

As previously mentioned JI composts are suitable for the majority of plants excluding, of course, those which require lime-free composts. When deciding which compost to use, a factor to take into account is the conditions in which the plants are to be grown.

When plants are grown on capillary watering trays, the compost is much damper than it is when the plants are watered at the top, hence it is desirable to have a compost with a more open texture. This is done by increasing the proportion of peat and sand in the mix. A compost which has proved very suitable for plants growing on watering trays is made up as follows.

Compost E6
3 standard seed trays of fibrous loam.
2 standard seed trays of peat.
1 standard seed tray of coarse horticultural sand.
6 oz (170 g) John Innes base.
¾ oz (21 g) hoof and horn meal.
¾ oz (21 g) bone meal.
1½ oz (42 g) powdered chalk.

This compost is suitable for most plants for all stages from the first potting up to their final potting.

Two other composts are recommended for certain plants in the text as follows.

Compost E2
1 standard seed tray of fibrous loam.
1 standard seed tray of peat.
1 standard seed tray of leaf mould.
1 standard seed tray of coarse horticultural sand.
6 oz (170 g) John Innes base.
2 oz (57 g) hoof and horn meal.
No chalk.

Compost E3
2 standard seed trays of fibrous loam.
2 standard seed trays of peat.
2 standard seed trays of leaf mould.
2 standard seed trays of coarse horticultural sand.
8 oz (227 g) John Innes base.
1 oz (28 g) hoof and horn meal.
1 oz (28 g) bone meal.
1 oz (28 g) powdered chalk.

In the event of being unable to obtain leaf mould use peat, which will in effect double the amount of the peat in the mix. The main difference between composts E3 and E6, when no leaf mould is present, is the ratio of loam to peat and sand and the quantity of chalk in the mix. Compost E3 is more open and more suitable for plants which prefer slightly acidic conditions (about pH6), such as gloxinias and fuchsias.

Greenhouse horticulture involves a considerable amount of potting and repotting and a very necessary and useful requirement is a portable potting bench. This can very easily be made by anyone capable of sawing and nailing.

All you require is 4½ ft (1.4 m) of 6 × 1 in (15 × 2.5 cm) planed timber and 4½ ft (1.4 m) of 6 × ½ in (15 × 1.3 cm) planed timber. Cut each piece into three lengths of 18 in (45 cm) and, using the 1-in (2.5-cm) thick wood for the bottom, make a three-sided open top box, using the ½-in (1.3-cm) wood for the sides. It is quite satisfactory to use nails, but if you are a perfectionist you may prefer to use screws to fasten the pieces together. To complete the portable potting bench the corners of the side pieces should be sawn off at the open end. This is a most useful piece of equipment as it can be used anywhere both outside and inside. You can, for instance, put it on a greenhouse bench, and instead of getting compost all over the bench it is all contained. When you have finished potting, any compost left over can easily be tipped back into the compost bag.

SHADING

During the spring and summer months it is essential to protect plants in the greenhouse from the direct rays of the sun. On a cloudless day, when the sun is shining continuously, the temperature in the greenhouse can easily reach 100°F (38°C) and more, and when this happens many plants are losing water, by transpiration, at a faster rate than it is being replaced, with the result that the leaves become limp and the plants droop. In this condition the direct sun scorches the leaves, causing considerable damage to the plants.

By providing the greenhouse with adequate shading the temperature in the house is kept to a lower level, and the plants are also protected from the direct rays of the sun.

When choosing a method of shading it is necessary to bear in mind that there can be as many dull grey days as there are sunny days in an average spring and summer, depending on your local climate. If the shading is too heavy this would result in the plants receiving inadequate light for satisfactory growth on dull days, and if the shading is too light, it would not fulfil its purpose on very sunny days. A material which answers the purpose admirably is a very fine mesh plastic netting, green in colour, often sold in rolls 2½ ft (75 cm) wide. It is not difficult to devise a method of hanging this on the inside of the greenhouse roof and sides. The method I adopt is to fasten a wire along the inside of the greenhouse eaves and, after securing the netting to the underside of the roof, using spring-type clothes pegs, it is then passed over the top of the wire and down the side of the greenhouse. In a 10 ft (3 m) wide greenhouse the netting is not wide enough to extend from the roof ridge, over the wire running along the eaves, and down the side of the greenhouse to the level of the bench; so I join two pieces together by threading thin coated wire through the holes in the netting at about 3-in (7.5-cm) intervals. This type of plastic netting can be used outside the greenhouse, which might prove more convenient to some greenhouse owners, as it is quite impervious to the weather.

Fine-mesh plain white net curtain material is also very good for shading, and protects the plants adequately while allowing a good light to reach the plants on dull grey days.

The greenhouse should be shaded from early spring until early autumn.

PLANNING

To get the best use of a greenhouse it is necessary to be systematic, which means that the year's work needs to be planned. There are many jobs each year which are repeated more or less at the same time. What these jobs are depends on the plants you are growing, and this, of course, will vary from one individual to another. If you are growing a fairly wide range of plants it is really a necessity to write out a programme showing the dates for sowing seeds, taking cuttings, starting tubers and bulbs etc., repotting and pruning. This not only ensures that these jobs are done at the correct times, but it also enables you to plan your work week by week.

Mediocre plants do not give much pleasure either to the grower or the onlooker, but a really well-grown plant is admired by all and gives the grower immense satisfaction. Pot plants require care and attention during the whole of their growing season and if they do not receive this at the time it is needed you will not get the best results.

Clivia miniata is an elegant plant which flowers in the spring.

GENERAL CULTIVATION OF POT PLANTS

It is not necessary to be a biologist to grow plants successfully, but it is much easier to understand the requirements of plants if you have some idea of how a plant functions. To grow plants in pots it is essential that you understand their requirements, because failure to provide the right conditions will usually produce a very disappointing result, and in extreme cases the plant will not survive.

Light, air, water and heat, together with potassium, nitrogen, phosphorus and trace elements, constitute the main requirements of plants and are all we need to be concerned with when dealing with the cultivation of plants.

It should be understood, however, that a plant is a very complex structure, and although the way it functions has been the subject of considerable research for very many years there are many processes involved in the growth of the plant which are still not yet understood.

LIGHT

Light is the plant's source of energy. It is like the electricity supply to a factory, and a plant can be likened to a chemical factory in so far as that in daylight hours it is constantly manufacturing the complex organic chemicals which are required for its growth.

In simple terms, when a plant is exposed to sunlight or daylight the rays of light are absorbed by chlorophyll, which is present in all green leaves, and this provides the source of energy which enables green plants to manufacture carbohydrates from carbon dioxide and water. This process is known as photosynthesis, and the speed with which it proceeds is, to some extent, dependent upon the quantity and quality of the light to which the leaf is exposed. The rays of light which are most important to the process of photosynthesis are red and blue. The green rays are, of course, all reflected, otherwise chlorophyll would not appear to be green to the human eye.

There is a limit to the speed at which the manufacturing processes can proceed, and above a certain light intensity no increase takes place. Similarly there is a minimum light requirement, and when the light intensity is below a certain level, such as a dull cloudy day in the middle of winter, photosynthesis slows down and may even stop, just as it does during the hours of darkness.

Although daylight is the source of energy, photosynthesis can only take place when the raw materials carbon dioxide and water are also available. The leaves of plants are so constructed that they can absorb air. The cells in a leaf are loosely packed and air can circulate freely between the cells. On the underside of a leaf there are thousands of special cells which are shaped like two sausages joined together at the ends. These two cells expand or contract, according to the existing conditions, thus opening and closing minute pores in the outer skin of the leaf, and this allows air to pass in and out of the leaf. These pores are called stomata (a single pore is called a stoma) and they are extremely small and very numerous. Even a medium-sized leaf contains hundreds of thousands. If you can imagine that an area of leaf the size of a pinhead contains a few hundred stomata it will give you a better idea of how minute these pores are. Because they are like tiny mouths, which can be opened and closed by the plant, as the conditions dictate, the flow of air or gases can be controlled by the plant according to its requirements.

Air, which is predominantly a mixture of the gases oxygen and nitrogen, also contains several others. One of these is carbon dioxide which, on average, is present to the extent of about 0.3 per cent. The air circulating round the cells in the interior of the leaf is the plant's source of carbon dioxide. Also needed for photosynthesis is water, and the plant obtains this from the compost or soil by means of the roots.

If you examine the active growing roots of a plant under a magnifying glass, you will observe that near the growing tip of each root there is a section of root covered with thousands of minute hairs. In soil, which is not dry, all the soil particles are surrounded by a thin film of moisture. This moisture consists mainly of water which has fallen onto the surface of the soil and then slowly permeated the whole mass, in the process of which it dissolves minute amounts of the soluble salts which are present in the soil. Each particle of soil is covered with a thin film of this very dilute solution of chemical salts. The root hairs, which are in close contact with these particles, absorb this solution, which then passes into the roots and up the plant's main stem and side shoots to the leaves. The flow of this solution from the roots is brought about by a force known as root pressure, the nature of which is still not completely understood.

To recapitulate, the leaf obtains the carbon dioxide (CO_2) it requires from the air, which enters through the stomata, and it obtains the hydrogen and oxygen from the water (H_2O) which it receives from the roots. The water from the roots contains soluble chemicals containing the main elements required by the plant, which are nitrogen, phosphorus and potassium. The plant needs these three elements, in particular, to enable it to manufacture cellulose for the cell walls, as well as proteins, fats and other complex organic chemicals necessary for active growth.

In daylight photosynthesis takes place, as already described, and the carbohydrate sugar, which consists of carbon, hydrogen and oxygen, is produced in the leaves. The hydrogen is obtained by the action of photosynthesis splitting up water into its two components – hydrogen and oxygen. This results in a surplus of oxygen, which passes out of the leaves through the stomata, thus in daylight, while photosynthesis is taking place, the leaves are taking carbon dioxide out of the air and releasing oxygen into the air. (This is the opposite of human breathing which involves inhaling oxygen and exhaling carbon dioxide.)

All green plants need light for their existence, but they vary very considerably in their light requirements. A guide to a plant's light requirement is the natural habitat of the species. A plant which, in nature, grows in a shaded location, for example in a forest or a jungle, will grow in a window facing north, whereas a sun-loving plant will not thrive unless it is placed in bright daylight.

In general it is not advisable to expose any flowering pot plant to direct sunlight, from mid-spring to mid-summer inclusive, when growing behind glass, particularly in a greenhouse, where the plant is also exposed to a high temperature. When plants are left exposed to direct sunlight on a cloudless day the visible damage is usually leaf scorch which can be quite extensive.

A very good method of shading in the greenhouse is to use white fine-mesh net curtain which, in most metal greenhouses, can be fastened to the glazing bars with wooden spring-clip clothes pegs. The outlay may be a little expensive but the net curtain will last for years. An alternative is to buy a very fine mesh plastic netting. The big advantage of using this type of shading is that it does allow direct sunlight to reach the plant, but not long enough for it to damage the leaves. Because the sun is moving all the time the netting casts a moving shadow over the leaves. It will also be appreciated that on dull days netting such as this will allow more light to reach the plants than other forms of shading.

TEMPERATURE AND ATMOSPHERE

Plants are greatly influenced by temperature, because the complex chemical processes which are taking place in a plant both day and night are dependent on the amount of heat available. Plants vary very considerably in their heat requirements and here again their native habitat is usually a good guide. Alpine plants, for example, have very different needs to those of tropical plants. All plants have their maximum and minimum temperature requirements. The maximum temperatures are not often given in horticultural books, and this is not an aspect with which we need to be concerned as the plant does not usually suffer if the temperature is too high, but merely ceases to grow. The minimum temperature requirement is a different matter, because usually it represents the minimum temperature at which the plant will survive without suffering damage.

There is much inaccuracy in this field and the figures given in many publications are far too high; consequently one should seek these figures in several different sources, and the lowest figure given will usually be the true temperature the plant can survive.

The growth of a plant is also affected by the humidity of the air surrounding it. Fortunately many flowering pot plants are quite tolerant in this respect and will survive a warm dry atmosphere during the period they are in flower without suffering irreparable damage. On the other hand there are a few species which will not survive if the surrounding atmosphere is too hot and dry. A perfect example of this is the cyclamen which requires a moist atmosphere and ideally a temperature range of $50-60°F$ ($10-15°C$). Put a healthy cyclamen plant, in full bloom, into a centrally-heated room, averaging say $70°F$ ($21°C$) and the high temperature coupled with the dry atmosphere will usually prove detrimental to the plant in a matter of days.

The humidity of air is measured by an instrument called a hygrometer, which shows the relative humidity of the air on a percentage scale; 0 per cent is completely dry air and 100 per cent is saturated air. As the temperature of air rises, its water absorption capability increases; consequently, as the temperature rises the drier it becomes, unless the water content is being increased at an appropriate rate. To clarify this, if a given quantity of air at $35°F$ ($2°C$) is saturated when it contains 2 oz (57 g) of water, it would require 8 oz (228 g) of water to remain saturated at $70°F$ ($21°C$).

During daylight hours the stomata on the undersides of the leaves are open and air is flowing into the interior of the leaves and circulating round the loosely-packed cells, before passing out of the leaves. The manufacturing cells in a leaf have a layer of moisture on the outside walls, which absorbs minute quantities of carbon dioxide from the air; this passes into the cell and is used in conjunction with the hydrogen and oxygen of water (H_2O) to produce sugar (a carbohydrate). The water or, more accurately, the dilute chemical solution, which the plant takes up from the soil, by means of its roots, is used by the plant to fill the cells and vessels of the plant, and a tiny fraction of the total quantity of water is used in the manufacture of sugar in the cell. Much larger quantities of water are drawn up into the leaves than the plant requires and this excess water evaporates from the moist layer on the outside walls of the cells, being absorbed by the air, as it circulates, throughout the interior of the leaf. This loss of water vapour from the leaves is called transpiration.

It can be appreciated that, on a hot summer's day, when a strong sun is shining on the surface of a leaf, the rate of transpiration is very high and, when the point is reached that the plant is losing water at a greater rate than its intake through the roots, the sausage-shaped guard cells forming the stomata lose their rigidity and become soft and flaccid, thus closing the pores and reducing or stopping the flow of air.

The ideal atmosphere for most pot plants is air with a relative humidity of $45-70$ per cent which, incidentally, is the ideal humidity range for human beings. When pot plants are surrounded by warm dry air, such as the atmosphere of a centrally-heated living room, the rate of transpiration is far too high and consequently adversely affects some of the processes which are taking place in the plant. In some plants the tips of the leaves die and go brown, buds drop off, flowers wither quickly, leaves wilt and the edges turn yellow.

There are, of course, quite a few plants which will grow satisfactorily in warm dry air, because these plants have been accustomed to growing in these conditions in their natural habitat. Cacti and succulents are examples, but in general it is found that thick leathery-leaved plants will tolerate this type of atmosphere whereas thin-leaved plants require an increased humidity.

There are several ways of providing humidity, and these are described in detail on pp.$29-30$.

WATERING

Despite all that has been written about the subject of growing plants in pots, it is probably still true to say that more pot plants die from being overwatered than from any other single cause. Possibly the reason for this is the fact that it is impossible to lay down any hard and fast rules for watering, and, although advice can be given, until you are experienced it is only too easy to make the mistake of overwatering.

There are many factors which have a bearing on the frequency of watering and these have all to be taken into consideration. Plants require more water when they are making good growth in warm sunny weather than when the weather is cooler and growth is slower. Plants growing in pots in the greenhouse on a warm sunny day in early summer would usually require watering morning and evening, whereas in dull weather in early summer would only need to be watered every other day at the most. Similarly a plant growing in a centrally-heated living room in winter might need watering every day, whereas the same plant, if placed in a virtually unheated room, might only require water once every 5 – 7 days.

The frequency of watering is also very dependent on the proportion of root to compost in the pot, as well as the size of the pot. All things being equal, plants growing in 3½-in (9-cm) pots require more frequent watering than plants growing in 5-in (13-cm) pots, but if there is only a small amount of root growth in the 3½-in (9-cm) pot, and the 5-in (13-cm) pot is full of roots, you would find the reverse to be the case, and it would be necessary to water the plant in the 5-in (13-cm) pot more frequently.

Another factor to be taken into consideration is the plant itself. Some plants require more water than others and, as a rule, thick leathery or fleshy-leaved plants do not require watering as frequently as soft thin-leaved plants. In any case the former will tolerate a drier compost without distress whereas thin-leaved plants usually wilt and droop as soon as the water supply is inadequate. Unfortunately a drooping plant is not always a sign that it requires water because plants also droop when they have been overwatered and it is this which makes it so confusing for the beginner.

Imagine that you buy a plant, bring it home and put it on a window-sill. The following day you think the surface soil feels dry, so you give it a good watering and, as the plant pot has been put in a decorative pot holder, the excess water drains into the holder, with the result that the plant is standing in water. This causes the compost in the lowest part of the pot to become waterlogged. Strange as it may seem, healthy soil or compost contains entrapped air, and without this air being present roots cease to function and die. When the compost becomes waterlogged it loses its air; consequently when pot plants are left standing in water the roots cease to function and begin to die. After a while the leaves begin to droop, because the roots are not working, and the leaves are not receiving any water to replace the water lost by transpiration. As soon as you see the plant beginning to wilt you think it must be short of water so you water it again with disastrous results.

In a case like this, when a plant begins to wilt a day or two after you have watered it, you can sometimes save the plant, if you realise it has been overwatered, by putting it in a warm position and allowing it to dry out completely. When the compost has dried out new roots will grow, if the plant has not been irreparably

damaged. During this drying-out process, the plant must not be watered at all, and if the leaves droop badly they should be sprayed with water using a fine spray.

Successful watering of pot plants consists of being able to detect when the plant needs watering and applying the appropriate quantity of water. It is, of course, better to water a plant before it shows obvious signs of requiring water, and when you become really experienced you can often observe that a plant needs watering just by the general appearance of the whole plant.

It is difficult to describe, but when you are familiar with a plant, having watched it grow for weeks on end, you can see a difference when it is just beginning to run short of water: it loses that robust, healthy look.

The main point, however, is to learn from your mistakes. Never water when the surface of the compost is damp. Do not always water when it feels dry, but be guided by other factors such as those already mentioned. Is the plant growing strongly? Is the pot full of roots? Is it a thick- or a thin-leaved plant? And so on.

Not many growers still use clay pots, but if the plant happens to be in a clay pot you can ascertain whether it is short of water by tapping the side of the pot with a piece of hardwood. If this produces a ringing sound, the plant needs water, but if it produces a dull thud it does not.

The best way to test a plant growing in a plastic pot is to grasp the rim of the pot between the thumb and the forefinger and 'feel' the weight, by lifting the pot up and down. This will not convey much to you at first, but if you make a regular practice of feeling the weight of pots, in this way, both before watering and after watering, you will, in the course of time, find it an excellent guide, but it does require a considerable experience.

Watering in the summer is not very difficult, and the time to water is usually when the surface of the soil feels dry. The plant will no doubt be growing strongly, the rate of transpiration will be high if it is an average summer temperature, and providing the plant is not left standing in water there is no chance of it being overwatered, by a correct application of water. It is, however, during the late autumn, and winter in particular, that the correct watering of plants becomes difficult. During this period there is another point to bear in mind and this is connected with the cycle of a plant's growth.

Many plants have a short resting period after they have flowered and during this period their water requirement is very small. In general most plants tend to grow most strongly when approaching their flowering time and it is during this period that they should not be allowed to become short of water.

Plants which bloom in the autumn and winter will consequently require watering more frequently, during this period, than plants which flower in the summer, as these are usually growing very slowly, if at all, during the autumn and winter months. Much has been said and written about the correct way to water a pot plant. Should it be watered from the top or the bottom? Either way is satisfactory but if you water from the bottom, by standing the pot in $1-2$ in ($2\frac{1}{2}$-5 cm) of water for a long enough period for it to penetrate the whole of the compost, you then have to allow the excess water to drain. When this excess water drains out of the compost it takes with it some of the soluble salts, which are always present in a good compost, and which the plant needs for its growth. If you make a regular practice of watering by this immersion method you will, in time, leach most of the soluble salts out of the soil and thus deprive the plant of its essential chemicals. This is the big disadvantage of the method of watering plants from the bottom.

Watering pot plants from the top by means of a watering can, with a long thin spout, is the easiest and the most satisfactory way of watering pot plants in the house. A thin spout is desirable because this delivers the water to the compost in a fine jet which can easily be controlled. This is important when watering plants such as cyclamen, *Primula malacoides* and saintpaulias, as the jet of water must be directed away from the crowns or centres of these plants. They have a tendency to rot if the crowns are allowed to become and remain wet. Cyclamen are particularly prone to rot, in the centre of the corm, when it is planted below or just level with the surface of the compost, and the leaf and flower stems are very numerous and crowded. In this case it is almost essential to water by the immersion method in which case the loss of soluble salts should be kept to a minimum by standing the pot in a shallow container holding a minimum quantity of water. Leave the pot standing in the water for two or three hours, as it takes much

longer for the compost to absorb the water in these conditions. If you have gauged the amount of water correctly there should be very little excess to drain away.

Much more could be written about the subject of watering but the foregoing will give you some idea of the complexity of this aspect of pot plant cultivation.

It will be appreciated that certain facts, as already detailed, have to be taken into account when deciding whether a plant needs watering. Let us take a typical example. You have, say, a Regal pelargonium, in flower, growing in a $4\frac{1}{2}$-in (11.5-cm) pot. The plant, being in flower, in this size of pot would usually be about $10-12$ months old, and the pot would be full of roots. You look at the surface of the compost and it is dry. You look at the plant as a whole and it looks healthy and robust. The flowers are beautiful and the petals are not showing any signs of flagging. You 'weigh' the plant in your hand in the manner described and it does not feel light. The plant does not need watering even if the compost does feel dry to the touch. If in doubt leave the plant until the end of the day and if it is still looking happy leave it until the following day.

In the case of a regal pelargonium, the first signs of water shortage are the flower petals beginning to droop. In other plants it may be the leaves which droop first. As you grow the various plants you will learn their different characteristics.

Finally, there is the actual watering. Plants which have been potted correctly have the surface of the compost about ¾ in (2 cm) below the rim of the pot, and when watering with a watering can cover the surface of the compost with water to a depth of about ½ in (1.3 cm) or just below the rim of the pot. If the plant needs watering, it is not likely that there would be any surplus water running out of the drainage holes in the bottom of the pot, unless the compost had become too dry, in which case the water just runs through the compost without really wetting it. When this happens it pours out through the drainage holes much quicker than surplus water from a properly watered compost. This is more likely to happen with a soilless compost which shrinks when it dries, leaving a space between the compost and the side of the pot. In cases like this it is necessary to stand the pot in water, as deep as the compost in the pot, and leave it to soak for a while until the water has permeated the whole of the compost, then allow the surplus water to drain away. Of course, plants should never be allowed to dry out as much as this, but it does sometimes happen with plants purchased from a florist or a supermarket, particularly with azaleas.

FEEDING

For healthy growth, plants need a steady supply of food, in the form of chemicals which, of course, must be in solution otherwise they could not be assimilated by the plant. The main elements required, apart from carbon, hydrogen and oxygen, which as we know the plant obtains from air and water, are nitrogen, phosphorus and potassium. In addition the plants also require very small quantities of certain other elements, mainly manganese, magnesium, iron, molybdenum, boron, zinc and copper. Because only minute quantities are required of these elements they are referred to as trace elements.

Vegetation in general does not usually suffer any shortage of trace elements because these are usually present in the soil in sufficient quantities. Also the commercial chemicals used in the manufacture of fertilisers very often contain trace elements as impurities; consequently when these fertilisers are used the necessary trace elements are supplied at the same time. Certainly when making up composts it is never necessary specifically to add any trace elements, and the pot plant grower need not be concerned with this aspect of the plant's requirements, as it will be well catered for in the course of feeding the plant with the main elements it requires.

The feeding of plants is similar to the watering of plants in that you have to take certain factors into consideration in order to know when to feed a plant and the type of fertiliser to use. Plants which have been potted in a good soil-based compost such as JI No.2 will not usually require feeding for at least three months. If a plant is potted on into a 5-in (13-cm) pot, say, from a 4-in (10-cm) pot, or from a 4½-in (11.5-cm) pot into a 6-in (15-cm) pot, it will not require feeding for a further six to eight weeks.

On the other hand a soilless compost contains much less plant food, and, in this type of compost, plants will usually need feeding about six to eight weeks after potting.

The modern gardener has a very wide choice of fertilisers, and it is therefore all the more necessary to have some idea of the purpose served by all these different mixtures. Nitrogen (N) is the element required for the growth of the green leaves and stems. Phosphorus (P) is the element required for healthy root growth. Potassium (K) is the element required for the production of flowers and fruits. It also promotes ripening of green stems giving strength to the plant structure. Too much nitrogen and too little potassium produces soft lush growth and stems with insufficient strength to support the leafy growth and keep the plant erect.

The best fertilisers to use for pot culture are liquid fertilisers or water soluble crystals, powders or granules. The relative amounts of the three main elements are always shown on the label of a fertiliser, and the important point to note is that the elements are always shown in the same order: nitrogen, phosphorus and potassium.

The relative quantities are calculated as the amount of nitrogen (N), phosphorus pentoxide (P_2O_5) and potassium oxide (K_2O) which are present in the mixture. Sometimes the full NPK analysis is shown, including the trace elements. Sometimes it merely gives numbers such as 'Formula 25:15:15', which means 25 per cent N, 15 per cent P_2O_5, 15 per cent K_2O.

John Innes base, which is the mixture of chemicals added to the soil, peat and sand to make up a John Innes compost, has the following content: 5.1 per cent N, 8.2 per cent P_2O_5, 10 per cent K_2O.

John Innes potting compost is made up in three different strengths (see p.13); therefore it depends to some extent on which strength has been used as to when the feeding should commence. No useful purpose is served in feeding a plant unnecessarily and more harm than good will be done by overfeeding, especially if this is done by applying the fertiliser in too concentrated a solution. When making up solutions of fertilisers always ensure that the quantities used are in accordance with the manufacturers' instructions. For the most part the type of fertiliser to use is a general purpose feed which has a balanced NPK content. Other than this the one to use will depend on the purpose for which it is required. If you wish to stimulate leaf growth use a high nitrogen mixture such as 25:15:15; and if this is being applied to a flowering plant you should change to a high potassium mix, such as 10:10:27, when the buds are well formed and beginning to show colour. The question of how often to feed cannot be determined without taking all factors into consideration.

A perennial-flowering pot plant, which has been potted at the beginning of its growing season, will only require feeding about five or six times, about every seven to ten days, commencing usually when the flower buds are beginning to form and ceasing two or three weeks after the flowering is over.

On the other hand, a permanent house plant, which has not been repotted or potted on, will require feeding about once a fortnight during the whole of its growing season, i.e. when it is growing strongly. It should not be fed when growth is very slow, usually during the few weeks before and after the winter solstice.

Some house plant growers prefer to feed their plants every time they water them, using a half-strength feed, and this is quite an effective way of meeting the plant's requirements. It should be pointed out that if a plant has been allowed to become too dry, due to an oversight, to the extent that it is showing signs of distress, it is not considered advisable to feed it in this condition. On occasions such as this it should be watered first and fed when it is next due to be watered again.

Finally, the important point to remember is that, as in the case of watering plants, it is far better to underfeed than to overfeed. Plants which are grown in a good compost such as compost E6 need very little extra food during a season's growth and many plants will give excellent results without any extra nutrients. It is usually only plants which make a lot of growth in a short period of time which really benefit, because they need the extra nutrients to keep pace with their growth.

PROPAGATION

There are two ways of propagating plants; one is by seed (sexual) and the other is by vegetative (asexual) methods. The latter vary, but the most common method involves cuttings. Plants which have been propagated from seed may be very similar to their parent plant or plants but they are never identical, whereas plants which are propagated by vegetative methods are identical to their parent plant in every way.

SEEDS
There is something very satisfying in raising new plants from seed, and although one's efforts are not always successful this is not necessarily the grower's fault. Consequently, do not be discouraged if, on occasions, seeds fail to germinate despite the fact that you have done all the right things. Before now I have sown two packets of seeds, being different varieties of the same plant, in the same seed pan; half the seed pan to each packet. The seed pan was enclosed in a plastic bag and placed in a heated propagator. One variety germinated very well whereas only one seed of the other variety germinated. As these seeds were varieties of the same species and were subjected to identical conditions, one can only conclude that one of the packets contained sterile seed, for one reason or another, not necessarily the fault of the seed growers. The point is that, although the seed growers make every effort to provide gardeners with viable seeds, there are occasions, and these are more frequent than you might think, when poor germination or complete failure is not the gardener's fault.

On the other hand by far the majority of failures are due to incorrect sowing methods. Perhaps the main cause of germination failure is making the seed compost too wet, which causes the seeds to rot, especially if the seed pan is enclosed in a plastic bag, which effectively prevents the escape of any moisture.

The sowing compost should be moist enough to obviate the necessity of watering again before germination is complete, but on the other hand it must be free from any excess moisture. For most sowings a 4½-in (11.5-cm) plastic half-pot is a suitable container. Fill this with the sowing compost, lightly compressing it, to make the compost firm, leaving the surface of the compost about ¾ in (2 cm) below the rim of the pot. It should then be placed in water about 2 in (5 cm) deep until the water appears on the surface of the compost. Allow the excess water to drain from the pot, then put it in your heated propagator for 24 hours, after which the compost should be in the right condition for you to sow the seed. A useful gadget for firming the compost in pots and seed trays can very easily be made from 1-in (2.5 cm) thick wooden board. Cut a piece measuring 3½ × 2 in (9 × 5 cm) and then cut one of the corners off, cutting about ½ in (1.3 cm) from the corner. Hammer a 1½-in (4-cm) nail into the middle of one side of the wood to serve as a handle. This can be used for firming the compost in any size of container from a 2½-in (6-cm) pot upwards, and also for seed trays, by using the flat side or the edges, according to the container.

A good guide to follow, when sowing seed, is the size of the seed, as this gives you some idea of the depth at which it should be sown. Seed should be sown at a depth which is about three times the diameter of the seed. A seed measuring ⅛ in (33 mm) should be sown ⅜ in (1 cm) deep. Very fine seed should be sown on the surface and not covered with any compost. A good method with fine seed is to spray the surface of the compost with a mist spray, after sowing, which helps to settle the seed into the surface of the compost.

Seeds vary in their temperature requirements, and these are always shown on the seed packet or in the seed catalogue. After sowing, place the pot in a propagator, at the correct temperature, either enclosed in a plastic bag or covered with a sheet of glass, to prevent the surface of the compost drying out. From time to time examine the pot for germination, and as soon as the seedlings begin to appear remove the covering and ensure that the seedlings are exposed to a good light. When germination appears to be complete remove the pot to a cooler temperature, say about 10°F (5.5°C) less than the germination temperature, to ensure sturdy growth, as too high a temperature will cause the seedlings to grow too 'leggy'. Some seeds germinate within a few days whereas others take several weeks. When sown at the correct temperature, coleus seeds will germinate in some six to eight days whereas cyclamen seed takes four to six weeks at the earliest, some of the seeds taking as long as eight weeks and more.

Seeds which are large enough to handle can be sown by placing each individual seed by hand on the surface of the compost, adequately spaced out, then covered with the appropriate amount of compost, preferably by riddling the compost through a fine sieve (a cook's household sieve is ideal for this purpose). When sowing seed which is too small to handle, it is a good idea to prepare a level surface by sieving a layer of fine compost on to the compost in the pot and very lightly firming this before sowing. This helps to keep the seed at an even depth.

There are various methods of sowing fine, to very fine, seed and all of them have their advantages and disadvantages. Perhaps the easiest is to sow straight from the packet. Cut the top off the packet, squeeze it to form a shallow trough, and while holding it at an angle keep tapping it with your finger to allow the seed to trickle out as slowly as possible. At the same time keep moving the packet backwards and forwards across the surface of the compost.

Whichever method you use it is inevitable, unless you are a genius, that when germination takes place you will get some overcrowding of the seedlings. These should be thinned as soon as possible, using a pair of tweezers, which enables you to pick up seedlings when they are very small. Even if germination has only been average, you will usually have many times more seedlings than you require, consequently you can thin the seedlings quite drastically to ensure that those that are left have adequate room for their development.

Fig.1 A household sieve is most effective for providing a fine level surface of sowing compost, necessary when sowing very small seeds.

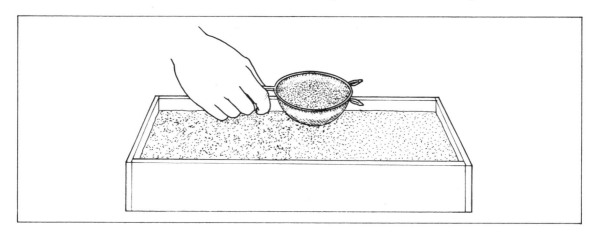

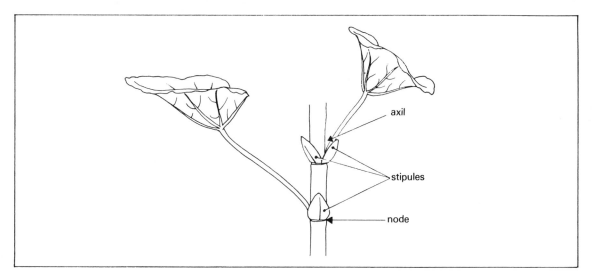

Fig.2 A stem cutting showing (a) the node which occurs just below the junction of the leaf stalk with the stem and is often apparent as a slight swelling on the stem; (b) the axil which is the upper angle between the leaf and the stem from which it is growing; (c) the stipule which is the leafy outgrowth at the outer base of the leaf stalk.

There are different opinions on the subject of transplanting seedlings. Some gardeners advocate transplanting the seedlings as soon as they are large enough to handle, whereas others are of the opinion that seedlings should not be moved until the first true leaves have formed. The first leaves which appear when a seed germinates are the seed leaves, after which the shoot continues to grow and the first true leaves then appear. The method I always use is to transplant as soon as the seedlings are large enough to handle. Using a plastic plant label, or a table fork, lift a portion of the compost, complete with seedlings, and separate the seedlings from the compost and from each other, being careful to avoid breaking the thin tapering roots. Handle the seedlings by their leaves only, and plant in 2½-in (6-cm) pots, or prick out into a seed tray, depending on your requirements. It is quite satisfactory, in fact it is advantageous, to plant the seedlings, even at this stage in their development, in compost E6 or John Innes potting compost No.2 or whatever compost they will finally be growing in. The seedlings should be planted to a similar depth to that at which they were already growing, never any higher but sometimes a little lower, especially if they look a bit drawn or leggy, through having been grown in too warm an atmosphere or too poor a light.

After transplanting, water the pots or seed trays, and keep them in a suitable place where they are receiving sufficient heat and light, but in all instances protected from direct sunlight, which would be detrimental at this stage.

CUTTINGS

When a gardener talks about a cutting he or she is usually referring to a stem cutting, and, in particular, a tip cutting, so called because it consists of the top 2 – 4 in (5 – 10 cm) of the stem, which includes the growing tip. It is very simple to take a stem cutting. All you have to do is to select a healthy stem and make a clean cut, through the stem, below the third node from the tip. (A node is a joint on the stem from which the leaf grows.) Remove all the leaves except the top two and also remove any stipules as these tend to rot and this can spread throughout the whole cutting. (A stipule is a leaf-like growth which is found on the stem at the nodes often growing round the base of the leaf stalk. These are very prominent on the stems of geraniums.) When the leaves have fallen off a stem the nodes can still be detected as a slight swelling on the stem.

It is essential that sufficient leaf area is left on the cutting to enable it to grow; therefore in some cases it may be necessary to allow more than two leaves to remain, if they are only small ones. It is really a question of striking a balance. The more leaf area there is on a cutting the more transpiration there will be, and as in the first instance the cutting does not have any roots the flow of water up the stem to the leaves is very slow, and too much leaf area will cause the cutting to wilt badly. This slows down, or may even prevent, the necessary chemical processes taking place; thus the cutting does not grow. On the other hand too little leaf area will have more or less the same effect.

To reduce transpiration, new cuttings should always be kept in a moist atmosphere. The easiest and most convenient method is to use rigid plastic domes, which can be obtained to fit various sizes of seed trays from half trays upwards, and there are also domes for 3½-in (9-cm) and 4½-in (11.5 cm) plant pots. A cheap but efficient way of covering a single cutting is to place an empty glass jar over it, the rim of the jar resting on the top of the compost. A 3½-in (9-cm) pot is the ideal size to use for this purpose.

Although it is not essential, particularly with cuttings which root easily, it helps to speed up the rooting process if you dip the base of the stem in a hormone rooting powder.

For success with cuttings the compost is an important factor. Ideally you require a compost which will remain moist, but not damp, as this would cause the cuttings to rot, firm enough to hold the cuttings in an upright position, even when they are being watered, and one which will encourage root growth and provide some food for the rooted cuttings. Many different cutting mixtures are recommended and, of all these, the one I have found the most satisfactory is a mixture of 3 parts of soilless cutting compost and 2 parts of fine vermiculite, by volume, well mixed together. There are numerous proprietary brands of soilless sowing and cutting composts and they all contain sufficient plant food, particularly phosphates. Vermiculite is expanded mica, and is an inert substance which will absorb and retain a considerable quantity of water. It has a twofold purpose in that it not only absorbs any surplus water from the soilless compost but also gives the compost a gritty texture. It has been shown that when roots meet with some resistance and have to force their way through the compost they develop more strength and become much sturdier. The vermiculite provides this resistance, and you find that cuttings grown in this mixture are appreciably bushier than cuttings which have been grown in a straight soilless compost.

Most cuttings will root satisfactorily in a minimum temperature of 65°F (18°C) day and night.

The light requirements for cuttings is the same as for the mature plants from which they have been

taken and it is essential to ensure that the cuttings are placed in as bright a light as possible, but shaded, of course, from direct sunlight.

As soon as possible the plastic covers should be taken off the cuttings, which will improve the light intensity. It is difficult to know when to remove the covers. Softwood cuttings, such as geraniums, fuchsias and begonias, should generally remain

Fig.3 When lifting cuttings it is important to avoid causing root damage. A wooden label or a spatula is ideal for this purpose.

covered for about seven to ten days. After this period, remove the cover and observe whether the leaves remain turgid after several hours' exposure; if not, replace the cover for a day or two until further tests show that they do. Using the cutting compost described, it will not usually be necessary to water the cuttings during the period they are covered by the plastic dome, but as soon as this has been removed the compost should be inspected daily to ensure that it does not become too dry.

One of the advantages of using this type of cutting compost is that the cuttings can be left growing in it for some six or seven weeks, and even longer, until they have developed a strong bushy root system. When the cuttings are well rooted, pot in 2½- or 3½-in (6- or 9-cm) pots depending on the size of the cutting, using the recommended compost for the plant being grown.

By far the majority of plants provide cuttings which root below the node but there are a few which provide internodal cuttings, a notable example being rhododendrons (which includes azaleas) and cuttings from these plants are prepared by cutting the stem halfway between two nodes.

Stem cuttings need not always be tip cuttings, and many plants such as dracaenas and dieffenbachias can be propagated by taking a section of the main stem, say 2 or 3 in (5 – 7.5 cm) long, containing at least two nodes, and treating it in the same way as a tip cutting. Providing there is a dormant bud to develop into a shoot, this method will provide you with a new plant; but it is a much more difficult way of raising plants than by tip cuttings, and the failure rate is very much higher.

There are other methods of vegetative propagation, such as root division, offsets, and plantlets, but these are peculiar to certain types of plants and are described, where applicable, in the plant section of the text.

POTTING

Plants grown from seed or from cuttings are initially potted in 2½-in (6-cm) or 3½-in (9-cm) pots but, as they continue to grow, the time comes when it is necessary to pot on into a larger size. By the time a plant needs potting on it has usually reached the point when its roots fill the pot, and it has used up most of the plant food in the compost. It is not difficult to know when a plant is ready for moving into a larger pot. The most obvious sign is when the plant begins to look too large for its pot. Another sign is when the roots begin to grow through the holes in the bottom of the pot, which usually, but not always, indicates that the pot is full of roots. Again, when a plant needs watering much more frequently, this also indicates a pot full of roots.

When this stage is reached, remove the plant from its pot and if there is a network of roots all round the outside of the root-ball, the plant is ready for potting on, but on the other hand, if the roots only look sparse at the bottom of the root-ball, keep the plant in the same pot for a while longer. If you find a mass of roots which have grown round the bottom of the root-ball, it means that the plant has been left in the pot too long and it is said to be 'pot-bound'.

One of the easiest ways of removing a plant from its pot is to place one hand over the surface of the compost, with the main stem between the fingers,

grasp the outside of the pot with the other hand, turn it upside down and gently tap the rim of the pot on the edge of the potting bench, or any solid surface. Do not attempt to remove a plant from its pot when the compost is dry, because firstly it tends to stick to the sides of the pot, and secondly if the plant is not ready for potting on the root-ball is liable to collapse and you will lose half the compost onto the bench, so if your plant is on the dry side water it a few hours before removing it from its pot.

Having established that the plant needs potting on, you have to decide which size of pot to use. To some extent this will depend on the plant you are growing. If it is a permanent foliage type of house plant the transfer should be confined to the smallest suitable size, which would be a pot 1 in (2.5 cm) larger in diameter, e.g. from a 3½-in (9-cm) pot to a 4½-in (11.5 cm) pot (potting from a 3½-in [9-cm] pot into a 4-in [10-cm] pot is not only difficult but it is quite unsatisfactory). The same remarks apply to slow-growing plants, whether foliage or flowering, as a pot 1 in (2.5 cm) larger will usually be sufficient for the rest of the growing season and further potting should not be necessary.

Some flowering pot plants and fast-growing plants, which make a lot of growth in a season, are better potted on into 5-in (12.5-cm) pots from 3½-in (9-cm) and if necessary their next move is into a 6-in (15-cm) pot.

As a general rule, however, select a pot 1 in (2.5 cm) larger in diameter when potting on.

Up to now we have been concerned with potting on, but another aspect to consider is repotting. A plant will grow in the same container, quite satisfactorily, for a long period of time, providing it is regularly fed, but there comes a time when, for various reasons, it ceases to thrive and begins to deteriorate. This could be caused by various factors but, whatever the cause, the only cure is to repot the plant. This is done by knocking the plant out of its pot and then, using a sharp pointed thin stick or preferably a steel knitting needle, loosen the compost from the roots. If you prod the root-ball all over then gently squeeze it between your hands, give a few more prods with the needle and then lightly shake it, you will find it possible to remove most of the compost from the roots. It does not matter if some of the roots are lost at the same time, providing a good root system still remains on the plant. You can then pot the plant into the same container using fresh compost when you will soon find a remarkable improvement in its growth. After you have repotted in this way the plant can then be potted on into a larger pot in due course if required.

A perennial plant which has been growing in the same pot for a whole season's growth should always be treated in this way, and not just potted on, if you wish to obtain the best results.

Thirty years ago everybody used clay pots. Nowadays all the professional growers supply their plants in plastic pots. Whichever type of pot you use it is quite unnecessary to put broken pot, gravel or any other kind of drainage material at the bottom of the pot, as recommended in so many gardening books and articles; in fact, when using watering trays or capillary matting, this can be detrimental. If you use the composts recommended, or soilless composts, these will drain quite satisfactorily. When using clay pots put a plug of fibreglass in the hole at the bottom of the pot; this will prevent any of the compost being lost and will also form a link between the watering tray and the compost.

Pots should preferably be washed before being re-used, unless you are repotting into the same pot.

GROWING PLANTS IN THE HOUSE

If you are a pot plant enthusiast you will want to grow pot plants, whether you have a greenhouse or not. It is, of course, much easier to raise and grow plants in a greenhouse than in a dwelling house; nevertheless, with a little equipment, it is possible both to propagate and to grow pot plants successfully in the house.

A standard size seed tray measures 14×8×2 in (36×20×5 cm). Transparent rigid plastic domes are made to fit over these trays, as a cover, and the best type is 5 in (12.5 cm) in height, with two ventilators in the top, which can be opened and closed. Electric heating bases are made which are approximately the same size as the tray; by fitting one of these underneath your tray, with a plastic dome on top, you have a miniature heated greenhouse. One of these on a suitable window ledge, which provides bright light, enables you to raise seeds and cuttings at any time of the year, according to the plant you are propagating. The electric heating base is usually rated at about 16 watts, which makes it very economical as it only uses a fraction more than 2½ units of electricity if it is switched on continuously for a whole week.

The bottom heat provided by these units is very beneficial when raising cuttings as it speeds up the growth and the cuttings root much more quickly. Because the cuttings are totally enclosed under the plastic dome, and the compost is being warmed by the heater, which causes evaporation of water, the atmosphere under the dome is ideal for them, particularly during the period before the roots have developed.

When using a propagator of this type it is better to have the cuttings and seeds in their own containers, which can be placed on the propagator seed tray, rather than filling the propagator seed tray itself with compost. You can use half-size seed trays (two of which will fit into a standard seed tray), plant pots or half-pots. This makes the use of your propagator much more flexible.

One of the main difficulties of growing plants in the house is the dry atmosphere of heated rooms. Some plants are quite tolerant and will survive for long periods of time. These are usually plants which are grown for their foliage, such as the various marantas and dracaenas. Most flowering pot plants steadily deteriorate and can only be regarded as temporary residents of living rooms, unless special provision is made to produce conditions which suit them. This is done by surrounding the plant with a moist atmosphere.

There are different ways of doing this, but they all work on the same principle, which is to provide excess water which will evaporate into the air in the immediate vicinity of the plant, providing a sort of micro-climate of moist air round the plant.

Perhaps the most efficient method is to have several plants together. Using a tray of suitable size, cover the surface with a ½-in (1.3-cm) layer of small

Fig.4 A shallow tray of small pebbles or stone chippings lying in water to just below the level of the pebbles will provide moist air to plants, such as this Maidenhair Fern, when growing in the dry atmosphere of a living room.

pebbles, or stone chippings, and fill with water to just below the level of the pebbles. When you stand a group of plants on the tray, this increases the efficiency of this method because the moist air is trapped between the leaves of the plants.

A good method for a single plant is to stand the plant on an inverted clay pot saucer, or something similar, in a bowl, or any suitable container, which has a diameter several inches larger than the plant pot, then fill the bowl with water to just below the level of the inverted saucer so that the plant itself is not actually standing in the water.

There are, of course, other ways of providing the plant with moist air, and it is merely a question of personal choice as to which method you use.

Some people advocate spraying plants with water, using a mist spray, but this is not very efficient. Apart from the obvious drawback that the water which misses the plant will not do your furniture much good, it provides only a very temporary amount of moisture in the air which is insufficient for the plants' requirements. Of course, it you have a group of plants on a tray, misting is then a good idea because it augments the moisture from the tray and, providing you direct the spray towards the centre of the group of plants, you are not likely to wet the surrounds. Never use the spray when the plants are exposed to sunlight as this could cause damage to the leaves.

Another problem to contend with, when growing plants in the house, is the light. All green plants require light for growth and some require more light than others. Except for shade-loving plants the best light is diffused sunlight. Obviously windows facing due south will give the brightest light but, in the summer months, when the sun is shining in a clear sky, this position is far too hot for all plants, even when shaded, except for cacti or similar desert plants.

In late autumn, winter and very early spring, before the days when the sun's rays get too hot, a south-facing window is suitable for many plants, but during the other months of the year it is better to position the plants in windows facing west-south-west to north-west, and east-south-east to north-east, where you will get maximum light with minimum danger of damage from the sun's rays.

Plants which will thrive in the shade can be put in north-facing windows in the mid-spring to mid-autumn months and in east- or west-facing windows in the other months of the year.

All these suggestions are based on the house being in an open situation. If any of the windows are shaded by trees, or by other properties, you would need to use your own judgement. Such shading can, of course, be a considerable advantage; for example, a window facing south-south-west which is shaded by a tree until late in the afternoon, when the sun's rays are no longer harmful to the plant, would be suitable for most species of plants, always providing the tree is far enough away from the window to allow plenty of light into the room.

When using pot plants for decorative purposes in the house, you naturally wish to put them in different places in the room, other than the window-ledges, but, apart from a table near the window, there are few other places where the plant will be receiving sufficient light to meet its minimum requirements for growth. However, if you can provide the plant with suitable artificial light there is no necessity for it to be positioned near the window.

It is possible to purchase special fixtures for housing plants and providing them with suitable artificial light in the form of fluorescent tubes. These vary in size from large cabinets to one plant fixtures. If you are DIY-minded you can design and make your own, but in this event it would be wise to consult a qualified electrician for the electrical part.

The quality of the light is most important and it has been found that the two colours of the spectrum which have the most effect are red and blue/violet. Fluorescent tubes of the type 'daylight' and 'warm white' are suitable particularly if both are used. Daylight tubes emit a preponderance of blue rays whereas warm white emit a preponderance of red rays; consequently, if you have a two-tube unit and fit one of each you get the best quality of artificial light for the plant, other than using the special 'plant growth' fluorescent tubes which are available but not always easy to obtain. If you are only using a one-tube fixture the best tube to fit is a warm white.

Ideally the fluorescent tubes should be suspended about 12 in (30 cm) above flowering plants and 24 in (60 cm) above foliage plants for the best results, but even if they are two or three times further away from the plants they are still beneficial, particularly when they are augmenting daylight.

In many, if not the majority of, homes, the incandescent electric light bulb is the most widely-used form of illumination, but unfortunately this is not a good source of light for plant growth, because light bulbs radiate too much heat; also the quality of light from a domestic light bulb is not as good. If the bulb is placed too near the plant it will scorch the foliage, whereas if it is placed at a safe distance the quantity of light reaching the plant is insufficient.

On the other hand, in my experience, the presence of wall-lights fitted with two 60-watt bulbs, about 2-2½ ft (60−75 cm) above a plant, illuminated for five to six hours each night, during the darker months, in conjunction with the amount of daylight it receives each day, is sufficient to keep a flowering plant in good condition for several weeks, while it is blooming, or a foliage plant for several months.

Most people have table lamps, standard lamps or wall-lights in their homes, and these can be used as a source of light for plants, thus making it possible to grow plants away from the windows for periods of time.

Because plants vary in their light requirements, some plants will thrive in places where other plants will rapidly deteriorate, and you have to find out by experiment the best situation for each species of plants. Try the same species of plant in different places in the house until you find the best one for that particular variety of plant.

Flowering pot plants are much more difficult to cultivate successfully in the house than foliage plants, but it is very beneficial if during the summer months they are put outside when not required for house decoration. The plants should be placed in a sheltered situation, where they are exposed to early morning or late afternoon sunlight. Flowering plants such as pelargoniums, fuchsias, lantanas and begonias, in particular, will benefit enormously from this treatment. Winter and spring flowering plants such as azaleas, cyclamen, cinerarias and all the primulas should be kept outside during these months.

Plants which are placed outside in the summer may be exposed to rain, and this should keep the leaves clean; but during a dry spell, or when plants are growing in the house, you should clean the leaves at least once a month. A simple way of doing this is to use a small wad of paper kitchen towelling which has been soaked in water containing a splash of washing-up liquid. Place the palm of the hand under the leaf for support, and wipe the surface of the leaf with the wet paper held in the other hand. When all the leaves have been treated in this way, go over them again with a paper wad soaked in clean water. Throughout the whole process keep re-arranging the surface of the wad of paper when it becomes dirty.

This treatment will improve the appearance of your foliage plants, but it will not be so noticeable with the flowering plants. The primary purpose of cleaning the leaves is not to improve the appearance but to remove the layer of dust, which if allowed to grow too thick would impede the light rays, which are essential to the growth of the plant.

In conclusion, it should be mentioned that from time to time it is a good idea to examine each plant closely, particularly looking underneath the leaves and at the growing points, to make sure that it is free from pests and diseases.

ACHIMENES
(Family Gesneriaceae)

The hybrid achimenes plants which are grown today are derived mainly from the species *Achimenes longiflora*, a native of Mexico. One of the most successful raisers of modern hybrids is Mr Konrad Michelssen of Hamburg, who has specialised in breeding new hybrids for many years.

Achimenes are grown from rhizomes or tubers, which are scaly in appearance. The fleshy scales are arranged in the manner of a closed pine cone and each scale is capable of propagation, but in practice one usually uses the whole tuber. Healthy plants usually produce several new tubers in a season's growth, so once you commence growing these plants your main difficulty is restraining yourself from growing too many plants. Select the biggest and most healthy-looking tubers for the next season's growth and discard the rest if you are unable to give them away.

Achimenes are beautiful plants which have a long flowering period, particularly if the tubers are started into growth in mid-winter. The flowers, which are usually available in violet, pink, red and blue shades, are 1½ – 2½ in (4 – 6 cm) across, and although each individual flower only lasts a few days new flowers are continually opening, giving a constant succession. Each individual flower consists of a tube, growing from the flower stalk, which flares out into five flat petals. As the colours are bright shades against an attractive green background achimenes are very decorative plants.

CULTIVATION

Tubers can be started into growth any time from mid-winter to mid-spring, but as they require a minimum temperature of 60°F (15°C) during the growing period the time to start them will depend on the amount of heat you have available.

Using compost E6 place the tubers on their sides and cover with ½ – 1 in (13 – 25 mm) of compost. Allow three tubers to a 4-in (10-cm) pot or five to six to a 5-in (13-cm) pot. Water the pots at the time of planting and only water again when it is absolutely necessary, i.e. when the surface of the compost is really dry. Start the pots in a propagator in a temperature of 65 – 70°F (18 – 21°C) until the shoots

appear, after which the plants can be moved to a slightly cooler place. A temperature of 60°F (15°C) is ideal.

When tubers have been started in mid-spring, by the time the shoots have appeared the greenhouse day temperatures will be averaging the required temperature for growth and, providing the night temperatures do not drop below 45°F (7°C), the plants will thrive quite satisfactorily.

The modern hybrids usually form bushy and compact plants but, should any stems appear to be growing 'leggy', do not hesitate to nip out the

Achimenes 'Rumpelstiltskin' grown from tubers. There are many varieties available in a wide range of colours.

growing tip. Other than this the plants do not need any attention, apart from watering, until they have flowered. When grown in a greenhouse they should be lightly shaded on bright sunny days in the summer.

After the plants have finished flowering, or by the middle of autumn, cease watering and ensure that the compost dries out completely. As the compost dries, the leaves will die off the plants and when the stems are obviously dry and dead they should be removed. Providing the compost in the pots is completely dry, the tubers can be left in the compost until the following season.

The pots should be stored in a minimum temperature of 45°F (7°C) during the winter months. If you cannot provide these conditions, remove the tubers from the compost and store in a cool place in the house. Achimenes should be grown in fresh compost every year.

Although achimenes are usually grown from tubers they can, of course, be grown from seed. The seed is extremely small and must not be covered by the sowing compost. Sow thinly on the surface of JI seed compost or similar, press the seed into the surface, then lightly spray with water using a fine spray. Sow from mid-winter onwards and keep the seed pan in a temperature of 65–70°F (18–20°C) covered with a sheet of glass.

Unless you have a greenhouse it is unlikely you will meet with success growing these plants from seed.

Achimenes can also be propagated from cuttings by selecting a strong shoot and taking a 3-in (7.5-cm) tip cutting, but as the plants produce so many new tubers each year there is not much point in propagating by this method unless you have a special reason for doing so.

AZALEAS – EVERGREEN
(Family Ericaceae)

Originally, when plants were being classified by Linnaeus in the eighteenth century, azaleas were treated as a separate genus, because at that time only deciduous species were known in Europe. Later, however, when evergreen species were introduced, botanists decided that all azaleas should be classified under the genus *Rhododendron*. It is to be understood, then, that when a nurseryman or gardener talks about *Azalea simsii* botanically speaking he is referring to *Rhododendron simsii*.

The fact that nurserymen and gardeners in general have continued to call these plants azaleas means you will usually find that most plant catalogues list azaleas separately from rhododendrons. To avoid any confusion, all the plants included in this chapter are described as azaleas in accordance with general usage.

There are about 70 species of azaleas and, in classifying these, advantage has been taken of a natural division, many of the species being deciduous whereas others appear to be evergreens because they retain some of their leaves throughout the year. For pot culture we are only concerned with the evergreen species and hybrids.

The first evergreen azalea to be introduced into England was apparently the Indian azalea *A. indica*

(or *indicum*) which was sent from China in 1808, and at that time was erroneously thought to be of Chinese origin, but actually it originates from Japan. This species was known in Holland as early as 1680 but was lost to cultivation for a long period of time, in fact

Azaleas bedded out in their summer quarters. The pots are sunk into the ground.

until 1768 when a batch was imported from Batavia. It was because this species was shipped from the East Indies that it was named *Azalea indica*, and by the time it was discovered that it was of Japanese origin the misnomer had become established, so today it is still called *A. indica* or *indicum*.

During the first half of the nineteenth century only a small number of evergreen azaleas reached Great Britain, but it was a very different picture during the second half of the century. This change was brought about by the many great plant-hunting expeditions which were organised during this period. In 1850 Joseph Hooker went collecting in the Eastern Himalayas and in 1855 Robert Fortune went to China. In 1899 Ernest Henry Wilson went to Western China and in later years to Japan.

All the evergreen azalea species originate in Eastern

Asia, mainly in Japan, China and Korea. The Japanese, in particular, have been cultivating azaleas for over 300 years; consequently most of the plants sent to England by the plant collectors were azalea hybrids.

During the second half of the nineteenth century evergreen azaleas were arriving in Britain, Belgium, Holland, France and Germany in ever-increasing numbers. Nurserymen and enthusiastic amateurs were engaged in cross-breeding hybrids and species on a large scale. By the end of the century there were over 1,000 named varieties of Belgian Indian azaleas, just one group of azaleas, which is an illustration of the extent of the breeding activities at this time.

There are some 40 species of evergreen azaleas, of which only about one third have been used in the raising of all the many thousands of different hybrids which have been grown.

Evergreen azalea hybrids are divided into groups, of which there are four of particular interest, these being Belgian Indian Azaleas, Kurume Azaleas, Kaempferi Azaleas and Glenn Dale Azaleas.

BELGIAN INDIAN AZALEAS

The azaleas in this group are sometimes illustrated and described in gardening books as *Azalea simsii* or *Azalea indica*, which is rather misleading because their origin is so complex that they cannot be related

Indian Azalea 'Leopold Astrid' is one of the many varieties of these highly decorative azaleas.

34

Kurume Azalea 'Hino-Mayo' is a very slow growing evergreen Japanese azalea which will flower in the winter.

to one species. It is less confusing if they are referred to as Indian azalea hybrids. The prefix 'Belgian' is often added because millions of plants are raised in Belgium every year of which about 85 per cent are exported.

This group contains some of the most attractive and beautiful flowers of all the evergreen azaleas, but the plants are not frost-hardy and need the protection of a greenhouse during the cold months of the year. All gardeners will be familiar with these plants as they are the azaleas sold by florists. In fact they are sometimes referred to as the 'florist's azalea'.

KURUME AZALEAS

The plants in this group are so named because they originated from the Kurume region in Japan. Kurume hybrid plants are usually bushy, and as they

are slow-growing make excellent pot plants which can last for 20 – 30 years before they become too big. They are frost-hardy and are, in fact, usually offered for sale as garden plants, and are readily available as named varieties. The flowers, which on well-grown plants completely cover the plant, are single or hose-in-hose.

KAEMPFERI AZALEAS

Amongst a batch of Kurume azaleas imported into Holland by a nurseryman called P.M. Koster some time before World War I was a plant of unknown origin. He gave it the name *Malvatica* and crossed it with the species *Azalea kaempferi* and this gave rise to the group called Kaempferi hybrids. Sometimes this group is called *Malvatica* or *Kaempferi × Malvatica*, but whichever name is used the plants are the same.

The plants in this group are similar to the Kurume hybrids but are more upright in growth and not as bushy. The flowers are in general slightly larger and bloom a week or two later in a similar colour range. They are quite as hardy as Kurume hybrids.

GLENN DALE AZALEAS

This is a very useful group because it contains some very beautiful varieties, and the blooming period is in late spring/early summer after the Kaempferi hybrids have finished. They were developed in the USA at the Plant Introduction Centre at Glenn Dale in Maryland under the direction of B.Y. Morrison. Hybridising began in 1935 and was carried out on a

large scale, some 70,000 seedlings being raised. Many different species and hybrids were used, so the plants in this group vary very considerably in growth, including low, medium and tall, upright or spreading.

Flowers are usually single, up to 4½ in (11.5 cm) across, but when pot-grown will usually be less than this. There were a few semi-double and double-flowered varieties.

The four groups described provide the grower with a wide range of colour and plants, but in addition there are many other azaleas which do not fall into these groups.

As already mentioned very many nurserymen were engaged in raising new hybrids, and quite often were successful in producing notable plants. It was quite a common practice for these to be known by the raiser's name. Such a man was Aart Vuyk, who in the early 1920s succeeded in breeding some beautiful hybrids. Many of his plants were named after famous musicians, such as 'Beethoven', but two of the most attractive were named after the raiser, namely 'Vuyk's Rosy Red' and 'Vuyk's Scarlet'. Both these make excellent pot plants as they are bushy, very slow-growing and have beautiful big flowers.

Another variety raised in Holland in a similar way, but without the knowledge of the raiser's name, is 'Sakata Red', which is also an asset to any collection.

When dealing with such a large class of plants as the evergreen azaleas, it is quite impossible neatly to place all the known hybrids into well-defined groups such as those described. It is quite likely that you will, from time to time, encounter plants such as 'Sakata Red' which are well worth growing, and you would require a very large greenhouse indeed to grow all the beautiful ungrouped azaleas which are available throughout the world.

CULTIVATION

The only way to start a satisfactory collection of azaleas is to buy young plants, which will usually be two or three years old except in the case of very small Belgian Indian azaleas. As azaleas can be lifted and potted at any time in the year, it is not necessary to purchase them at any specific time, but from your own point of view, it is more expedient to purchase your plant in the spring. By doing this the plant is settled in its pot and under your control at the time when it is making new growth and developing its flower buds for the following season.

It is crucial that the plant is given the cultural attention it requires during the late spring and the summer, for a successful show of bloom the following winter or spring.

Azalea 'Vuyk's Rosy Red'. The large brightly-coloured flowers of this type of azalea are always greatly admired.

However, assuming that you purchase a plant in bud during the winter to spring period it will, in the case of all varieties other than the Belgian Indian, require potting. For this purpose you can use either a plastic or a clay pot, whichever you prefer, but the important point is to use the smallest possible pot which will satisfactorily contain the roots. The reason for this is that azaleas are capable of living for very long periods of time, and by starting with the smallest size of pot you are increasing the length of time the plant can serve as a pot plant. All flowering pot plants benefit by being potted on into a larger size and this is particularly true of azaleas.

By starting with a small pot you increase the number of times it can be potted on. Ultimately it will require a larger pot than is practicable in order to continue growing satisfactorily, but by this time you will have enjoyed some 15 – 20 seasons of flowering. Azaleas are such permanent plants that you cannot help but get attached to them. I have a Kurume azalea called 'Hino-mayo' which I acquired about fourteen years ago, and it has become a rather special favourite with me. I usually force it into bloom in late winter and in some years it is completely covered with flowers.

A suitable compost for azaleas consists of:

> 1 standard seed tray of peat
> 1 standard seed tray of leafmould
> 1 standard seed tray of sand
> 3 oz (85 g) hoof and horn meal
> 2 oz (85 g) bone meal.

Leafmould is difficult, if not impossible, to obtain nowadays, and if it is not available use lime-free soil.

Pot the plant firmly and then water by filling the pot up to the rim. If the plant has been potted correctly the level of the compost will be about ¾ – 1 in (2 – 2.5 cm) below the level of the rim.

The Indian Azalea is one of the best winter-flowering pot plants.

The azalea should not require watering again for at least a week, assuming that it has been put in a cool greenhouse immediately after potting.

Azaleas thrive in a moist compost and should never be allowed to dry out. On the other hand no pot plant will survive a wet compost, such as the condition which exists when the pot is left standing in water for a period of time. It is necessary to strike a happy medium and in this respect you often can, in the case of azaleas, receive help from the plant itself, because the main stem turns a darker colour when the roots are well supplied with water. When the moisture content of the plant is ideal, the dark colouration of the stem ceases about 1 in (2.5 cm) above the soil level. When it is higher than this the compost is on the damp side, and when it is lower than 1 in, the plant should be examined daily until it has been watered. On some plants it is very easy to see the dark colouration, but not all plants give a clear indication; therefore you have to be careful, and if you cannot distinguish any difference in the colour of the stem do not jump to the conclusion that the plant is short of water. Use this guide in conjunction with the feel of the compost. If it feels moist, it obviously does not need watering whether you see a water line or not.

You should not expect good results from your plant as soon as it has been potted, as it needs to become established as a pot plant and to have grown in the right conditions for a season.

Even in the case of Belgian Indian azaleas you often find that the plant has suffered while on display waiting to be sold, and as they are invariably potted in a soilless compost it is not unusual for this to have become too dry. If this should prove to be the case the plant should be placed in a bucket or bowl of water so that the pot is almost immersed, to ensure that the compost receives a thorough soaking, and then it should be allowed to drain.

When the azalea has finished flowering it should be kept in a cool place where the atmosphere has a good moisture content, such as a cool greenhouse or a spare room in the house which is unheated or only partially heated. A temperature of $40-50°F$ ($5-10°C$) is ideal and will make the plant grow steadily assuming that the light is sufficient. Plants should not be kept in the living room or centrally-heated rooms for longer than the period they are in flower, usually some four weeks, as the atmosphere is too dry, and although they will stand limited exposure to these conditions a prolonged stay could damage a plant to the extent that it would take a long time to recover.

Although it is possible to grow azaleas in pots without a greenhouse it is, of course, far more satisfactory to grow them in a greenhouse, particularly if you have a collection of different varieties.

All varieties of azalea, except the Belgian Indian, should be removed from the greenhouse in spring and put in a sheltered spot where there is some protection from the frost. The Belgian Indian hybrids are not frost-hardy, consequently they need more protection than the other groups, and should be kept in the greenhouse until late spring when they can be removed to the protection of a frame or similar place.

All pot-grown azaleas should be bedded out in the summer and it is easier and quite satisfactory to keep the plants in their pots rather than planting them in the ground. The best site is one which is open to the sun for some three or four hours a day, preferably in the morning, and for the rest of the day in partial shade. It is not essential because azaleas will endure partial shade all the time or even full sun all the time, but in the case of azaleas in pots it is desirable for growth to be as dense and compact as possible. Partial shade all the time encourages taller and more open growth. Full sun all the time causes the pots to dry out far too quickly, and would necessitate watering too frequently.

Belgian Indian azaleas should not be bedded out until all risk of frost has passed.

The object of bedding out azaleas in the summer is to give them natural growing conditions which ensures that good strong healthy plants are developed. A good method to use is to dig a hole large enough easily to accommodate the size of pot involved, then place some peat at the bottom of the hole; stand the pot on this and then surround the pot with peat. The soil is then packed round the peat and made very firm to ensure that the pot is secure against the wind. The pot should be so placed that the ground level is about 1 in (2.5 cm) below the rim of the pot.

The use of peat as a lining round the pot is to prevent it coming into contact with the soil which may not be lime-free, also damp peat will retain the moisture better and reduce the amount of watering required particularly where clay pots are involved.

All the azaleas should have been bedded out by

early summer and this is a good time to give them an application of sequestrene (active ingredient iron chelate) which will suffice for the whole season.

A lot has been written about using rainwater for the watering of pot plants, particularly plants which require acid soils, and it is very good when you can do this. On the other hand, if you grow a large number of pot plants it is not always possible to collect enough water to meet their requirements. In my long experience tap water (unless it is 'hard') is just as satisfactory and I have never used any other source of supply, so do not worry if you have to use tap water for your azaleas, as they will not come to any harm, particularly if you give them the sequestrene treatment once a year.

The azaleas should be left bedded out until the end of the summer, when they should be lifted and put in a frost-free place. During early autumn they can be kept outside if given the protection of glass or a polythene cover, but by late autumn they should be inside the greenhouse. At this stage it is better if the greenhouse is unheated and the thermostat is set for say 36°F (2°c), just enough to keep out the frost. This ensures that the azaleas are growing in cool conditions, which is absolutely essential if they are to flower satisfactorily.

It is necessary for the plants to have a 'chilling' period i.e. below 50°F (10°C) for four to eight weeks, as it is during this period that processes occur which prepare the buds for flowering and, as a result, the buds all break into flower at the same time, as soon as a period of higher temperature is experienced. Without this period of 'chilling', flowering is often spasmodic over a long period of time and the azalea fails to give a good show of bloom.

When I first started growing azaleas in pots, this spasmodic blooming often occurred with my plants. I read somewhere that it was due to overwatering, so I began to water my plants very carefully, but of course it did not give the desired results.

It is often recommended that azalea plants should be sprayed daily with cold water, and no doubt this practice developed because spraying in autumn would result in chilling the plants, particularly on overcast days when the plants would remain damp for a few hours, if not all day. It is not however necessary to spray plants at all if the temperature is kept low by avoiding artificial heat and opening the vents on sunny days.

After the plants have been subjected to this 'chilling' period they are ready for forcing into flower, and this can commence at the beginning of winter or in late autumn if the weather has been cold enough during the early autumn. All that is necessary is to put the plant in an average temperature of 65°F (18°C), in a position where it is receiving good light. All plants need light, which provides the energy for growth, and as the object is to speed up the process of flowering obviously the plant must have good light as well as heat.

Ideally the plant should be put in a propagator which is heated to a steady 65°F (18°C). If this propagator is in the greenhouse the natural light will no doubt be sufficient to sustain growth. It is better, however, if you can provide the plant with artificial light, because there are many days in winter when the light intensity is insufficient to sustain growth. A 'warm white' fluorescent tube about 12 in (30 cm) above the plant for 12 hours per day, say 8 am to 8 pm, will make a considerable difference to the length of time required to bring the plant into full bloom. It is not essential to provide artificial light, nor indeed to have a propagator. The plant can be forced by placing it in a centrally-heated living room, in the window, or in any position where it will receive maximum light.

It is, however, desirable if you have a collection of azaleas, and wish to maintain a continuity of bloom, to be able to control the rate of forcing, and this can best be done if you can control the heating and lighting conditions.

Very few flowering plants will thrive inside the house because the air, particularly in centrally-heated rooms, is too dry. Azaleas are no exception, and five or six weeks in the house will begin to affect the plant. It will usually show this by shedding some leaves. This is another reason in favour of using a propagator, because the atmosphere can be kept moist.

On the subject of leaf shedding, it should be mentioned that although the azaleas with which we are concerned are called evergreen azaleas they are not evergreen in the true sense of the word. They do in fact appear to be evergreen because they grow two types of leaves. One type grows in the spring and the other in the summer. In the autumn they shed most of their spring leaves, and it is important to realise this; otherwise you might conclude that the plants are not happy when the leaves begin to die and fall off. It is a natural process and does not indicate that the plants need watering or a change of environment. On the other hand, by the time the plant has flowered all the spring-grown leaves have long gone, and a fall of leaves at this time would be of the summer leaves and indicates that the plant is in need of attention. The summer leaves are more permanent than the spring leaves and usually last until the following year, and in some species even longer.

In a temperature of 60–70°F (15–21°C) with good light, it takes about four to five weeks for the tight buds to open into flower. With a carefully-selected collection of azaleas you can start with the first plant in late autumn, and as soon as this is in bloom and ready to move into the house, the forcing of the next one is commenced, and so on until late spring, by which time it is unnecessary to force the plants.

The plant remains in bloom about the same length of time as it takes to force into bloom; consequently, when it begins to fade, the next plant is ready, and so a continuity is achieved.

Azaleas are possibly one of the most satisfying pot plants you can grow, because once you have started a collection you are never without flowering pot plants during the winter months.

A WELL-BALANCED COLLECTION
BELGIAN INDIAN AZALEAS

These are the best plants for forcing into flower from mid-autumn onwards. They are not usually sold as named varieties nowadays, but they are available in many shades of reds and pinks, and also as bi-colours such as pink with white edges. Ideally you need about ten to twelve plants to cover the six-month autumn to spring period. The most economical way to acquire a collection is to buy small plants, because the price increases with the diameter of the head of the plant. Granted it takes some four or five years for these to grow into impressive plants but, from then on, you can look forward to many years of undiluted pleasure. There is no more magnificent sight, in the pot plant world, than a mature evergreen azalea in full bloom in the middle of winter.

KURUME AZALEAS

These hybrids can be brought into flower in late winter and if kept in an unheated room in the house will remain in bloom for eight to ten weeks. Recommended varieties are: 'Hino-Mayo' – soft pink, single flowers; 'Hinode-Giri' – light red, single flowers.

KAEMPFERI AZALEAS

These bloom naturally a little later than the Kurume hybrids and should be forced into bloom in early spring. Recommended varieties are: 'Willy' – bright pink, single flowers; 'Orange Beauty' – soft orange, single flowers.

VUYK AZALEAS

These hybrids will force well in early spring and will bloom naturally in spring and are very striking. Recommended varieties are: 'Vuyk's Rosy Red' – bright red, single flowers; 'Vuyk's Scarlet' – deep red, single flowers.

GLENN DALE AZALEAS

These can be forced into bloom in spring or will bloom naturally in early summer. Recommended variety: 'Martha Hitchcock' – white margined with magenta, single flowers.

BEGONIAS – TUBEROUS
(Family Begoniaceae)

The plants we grow today are hybrids developed from species which originated in South America, such as the scarlet *Begonia boliviensis* from Bolivia; the rose *B. clarkei* from Peru; the orange-scarlet *B. davisii* from Peru; the vermilion red *B. veitchi* from Peru; and the primrose yellow *B. pearcei* from Bolivia.

The botanist monk Plumier is credited with discovering the first plants towards the end of the seventeenth century. As the plant could not be placed in any known genus, he decided to name the plant himself, a practice which was quite common in those days, and he named it after a man he admired, Michel

Begon (1638 – 1710), a French botanist, who at one time was the Governor of Santa Domingo.

The begonia was introduced into Great Britain in 1777, but it was many years before hybridists began to breed varieties on a large scale. At first only single-flowered hybrids were produced, but later semi-double and finally double-flowered varieties were achieved.

There have been many notable hybridists and nursery firms involved, and the raising of new cultivars has continued up to the present day, it will no doubt also continue for many years to come, for the very good reason that begonias are excellent greenhouse and bedding plants, as well as being very decorative house plants.

CULTIVATION

Begonias are grown from seed, tubers or cuttings. Usually most growers raise the plants from tubers, which are readily available, and once purchased can be grown on for several seasons. Having purchased the initial stock there is no further cost involved and the stock can easily be increased by means of cuttings, which are taken from the plants you most admire. By this means you can be sure of obtaining the varieties you require, whereas from seed you cannot be sure that the flowers will come up to your expectations.

Tubers should be started into growth in late winter or early spring. A good method is to fill a seed tray with peat and place the tubers in the peat, so that the top of the tuber is just covered by the peat. If you examine a tuber you will usually find that one side is rounded and the other side is concave or hollowed out. The concave side is the top and the tubers are placed in the peat with this side uppermost. By covering the tuber with peat you ensure that water does not lodge in the slight depression on the top side, because the peat holds the water. This is important because the tubers have to be kept moist to start them into growth, but on the other hand they tend to rot quite easily if they are too wet. It is for this reason that it is better to start them into growth in peat, rather than potting in compost in their final pots, as it is difficult to avoid having a soil compost too wet.

Begonias need a temperature of 60 – 70°F (15 – 21°C) to start into growth, and when the shoots are about ½ – 1 in (13 – 25 mm) long, carefully lift each tuber, which will also have made root growth, and pot in compost E3.

The size of pot to use is determined by the size of the tuber and should be such that there is about 1 in (2.5 cm) of space between the tuber and the side of the pot.

After potting keep the plants in the propagator at 60 – 70°F (15 – 21°C) until they are well established, and as soon as they are obviously making good growth move them to the greenhouse bench where you have a minimum night temperature of 50°F (10°C).

If the plants are kept in the propagator too long they will make lush sappy growth with very large leaves, which is not desirable. On the other hand they need a minimum temperature of about 50°F (10°C),

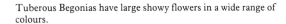
Tuberous Begonias have large showy flowers in a wide range of colours.

there are small buds on either side of the main bud. These are female flowers and they should be removed early to ensure a larger bloom.

Tuberous begonias usually bloom quite prolifically for some two to three months, but by early autumn or when flowering has ceased water should be withheld from the plants to allow the compost to dry out completely. As soon as the leaves have dropped, the stems should be removed by twisting off the tubers, but they should not be forced off. If they do not come off with a slight twist, leave until they will come off easily. It is essential to ensure that the compost is bone dry if you propose to store the tubers, as they are, in their pots; otherwise they will rot. If stored in this way, a minimum winter temperature of 40°F (4°C) will suffice. An alternative method of storage is to separate the tubers from the compost and store loose in plant pots or a similar type of container. Any cool dry place with a minimum winter temperature of 45°F (7°C) would be satisfactory.

As mentioned earlier new plants of tuberous begonias can be propagated by means of cuttings. When starting into growth you will find that tubers usually send up more than one shoot, and in the case of one-year-old tubers it is better to remove all but one. With older tubers you often get three or more shoots, and these should be reduced to two. When cuttings are required these shoots should all be allowed to grow until the stems are about 3 in (7.5 cm) long, and then they can be removed completely from the tuber. Prepare the cuttings in the usual way by cutting the stem just below a node and removing all but the top leaves.

Cuttings taken this way have all the growing season to build up a tuber and can be expected to produce a small flowering plant the following year. If, however, the tubers you wish to propagate do not oblige you with spare shoots, you will have to obtain your cuttings from side shoots as and when they develop on the main stem. Obviously you will have to wait several weeks for these to appear, with the result that half the growing season will have passed before you are able to strike the cuttings; they will consequently make much smaller plants in the first season than the cuttings obtained from the tubers.

give or take a degree, and if you have started the tubers into growth in late winter it will be the middle of spring before the plants will be ready for the greenhouse bench. It is not very costly to maintain the minimum temperature required at this time of the year, but should you wish to avoid the cost then the start should be delayed until the middle of spring. Ideal growth temperatures are 55–60°F (13–15°C) at night, and 70–80°F (21–27°C) by day.

Begonia plants require very little attention especially if grown on watering trays. Plants grown from one-year-old tubers should be confined to one shoot by removing all shoots other than the strongest one. When flower buds form it will be found that

43

BOUGAINVILLEA
(Family Nyctaginaceae)

Bougainvilleas are by nature climbing plants, but a number of hybrids developed from *B. buttiana* are less vigorous than the species and can be trained as bushy shrubs, or alternatively as compact plants on a wire hoop or a framework.

The common name of this plant is 'paper flower', which is a description of the coloured bracts formed when the plant blooms. The flowers are small and insignificant, but the large bracts which give the plant its very attractive appearance are brightly coloured and have a papery-looking texture.

Bougainvillea glabra will provide colour throughout the summer.

These plants are not easy to propagate but they are freely available, and although varieties occur with white, yellow, orange, pink, red or purple bracts it is usually the pink or red shades which are offered.

CULTIVATION

Plants are offered when in flower, during the late spring and summer months. Once the bracts have formed, and coloured, they should remain on the plant until the autumn.

During the summer the plant should be kept in a bright light, preferably direct sunlight, when inside the house or outside. On the other hand, if the atmosphere is too dry the bracts are apt to fall; consequently, if the room is heated, it is advisable to provide the plant with moisture either by spraying it

or by standing it on pebbles in a dish of water (or similar means of providing moisture).

When the bracts have faded or fallen, the plant should be put in the greenhouse, keeping the compost on the dry side, but watering sparingly from time to time. A temperature of 45−50°F (7−10°C) will suffice during the winter.

In spring repot the plant by removing as much of the old compost from the roots as possible (see pelargoniums for the method of doing this) and potting the plant in the same size of pot, if possible, but if it has grown too large for this then use the next larger size. Use compost E6 or JI No.3. At the same time the plant should be pruned. Cut out all the weak growth and reduce the strong growth by about a third.

If plants are repotted every year they do not really require any feeding, but a fortnightly feed with a balanced liquid fertiliser from mid-summer onwards is beneficial for plants which have not been repotted. After potting the plant should be watered, and from then on keep the compost well watered during the growing and flowering season, but do not allow it to get too wet.

BROMELIADS
(Family Bromeliaceae)

Bromeliads is the name given to a group of plants which mainly originate in South America. The group contains plants which are quite diverse in appearance, such as *Aechmea fasciata* and *Bilbergia nutans*. Several of the genera contain epiphytes, which in their native habitat grow on the trunks and branches of trees, obtaining their food from the air mainly through their leaves. Others are terrestial plants which grow in the ground obtaining their plant food through their roots.

Probably the most well-known bromeliads are *Aechmea fasciata* (urn or vase plant), *Vriesia splendens* (flaming sword plant), *Guzmania lingulata*, *Tillandsia lindenii*, *Bilbergia nutans*, *Ananas comosus* (common pineapple), *Neorogelia carolinae*, *Nidularium innocentii* and various species of *Cryptanthus*.

Of these the most unusual and striking are *Aechmea fasciata* and *Vriesia splendens*. As they are both very

Aechmea fasciata, the Urn Plant, is very striking when in full flower.

Vriesia splendens is known as the Flaming Sword, because of the appearance of its blade-like flowering spike.

good houseplants, a description of their cultivation will suffice as it is applicable to all the other epiphytic bromeliads.

Aechmea fasciata has arching spiny green leaves banded with grey in such a manner as to give almost a mottled effect. The flower is predominantly pink in appearance consisting mainly of bracts on a strong stem which grows from the centre of the plant. The actual flowers are small, blue and quite insignificant, lasting for only a short time, but the pink inflorescence made up of the bracts lasts for months under good conditions.

Vriesia splendens also has arching leaves, which are bright green, with dark bands running across the leaves. These bands vary in colour, in different plants, from dark-brown to purple-black. The flowers which are borne on strong stems are long and flat, and again it is the bracts which give the flowers their predominantly red colour.

46

Ananas comosus, the Pineapple Plant.

Both these species take about three or four years to flower, given the right conditions; they only flower once, then they die.

The leaves of both aechmeas and vriesias are arranged in a rosette and the leaves in the centre of the plant sheathe one another, forming a cup-like receptacle which is completely water-tight. When growing in the wild, rainwater collects in this receptacle, and any vegetable matter floating in the air, such as dying leaves, may fall into this from time to time. These plants obtain virtually all their plant food in this way, and the function of their small rooting system is to anchor the plants to the surface on which they are growing.

CULTIVATION OF AECHMEAS AND VRIESIAS

It is not recommended that the amateur should grow these plants from seed. Plants should be purchased preferably when they are coming into flower, as the

47

flowers last very well, particularly if they are kept in a cool atmosphere, say 50–60°F (10–15°C).

The plants prefer a bright light, but filtered rather than direct sunlight.

During the period early spring to early autumn, the cup in the centre of the plant should be kept filled with water, with an occasional feed with a weak solution of a general liquid fertiliser. Plants usually grow faster in the spring and autumn than in midsummer, and they have a resting period of about four months in the winter. If the plants are kept in the house in living room conditions, during the resting period do not allow the cups to run dry but keep a very small amount of water in them. Do not water the compost at all during this period. If the plants are kept in the greenhouse or cool house conditions, it is better to allow the cups to dry out and remain dry otherwise it may lead to rotting of the leaves.

The young plants will not usually flower until they are three to four years old and they may require high temperatures above 75°F (24°C) to induce them to flower; thus it will be appreciated that they require summer conditions in a greenhouse.

I once read somewhere that if a bromeliad of this

Billbergia nutans flowers from early summer to winter.

type is enclosed in a transparent plastic bag with a very ripe apple, the gas given off from the apple triggers off the processes which cause the plant to flower. Never having tried it, I do not know whether this works; but even if it does not it is still worth propagating vriesia and aechmea because they are very ornamental plants even when they are not in flower.

During the growing period the compost in the pot should be watered lightly from time to time but never allowed to become wet. It is better kept on the dry side.

If you live in a hard water district you should use rainwater for filling the receptacles in the plants, but this is not necessary in other areas where tap water is quite satisfactory.

After the plant has flowered it begins to die, but not before it has formed offsets at the base of the plant.

Neoregelia carolinae is a bromeliad and is watered by keeping the centre leaf cup full of water.

These offsets should be allowed to grow until they have developed the cup-like receptacles which are characteristic of the plant. By this time the leaves of the offset will be several inches long, and when carefully separated from the parent plant it will have a good root system of its own. The best time to propagate plants is early spring.

Pot the offset in a soilless seed and cutting compost, which is ideal for the whole life of the plant, bearing in mind that the main purpose of the compost is to support the plant. As for the size of pot to use, this should be governed by the size of the plant. Choose the smallest size which looks appropriate to give a good balance.

49

CAMELLIA
(Family Theaceae)

Camellias are flowering shrubs of which there are numerous cultivars and hybrids. These have been raised from the many different species introduced to Europe from China and Japan. Of the many different types available *Camellia japonica* hybrids are the plants usually grown for pot culture. They were very popular in Victorian times and many large estate owners devoted a whole greenhouse to their cultivation. Some magnificent specimens, bearing hundreds of flowers, were grown.

Actually *Camellia japonica*, and its hybrids, is quite hardy and can be grown outside with success in milder climates.

The propagation of camellias is difficult and best left to professional growers, so if you wish to grow these plants you will need to purchase your requirements from a nursery. Although the initial cost is quite high it should be remembered that they are slow-growing shrubs which will give you pleasure for very many years. Probably the best time to purchase your requirements is in the autumn because

at this time of the year you are able to see the dormant buds on the plants, and you can select plants which are well-endowed with flower buds. It is easy to distinguish between the flower buds and the leaf buds because the former are much rounder and larger in size.

Camellias are evergreen shrubs with beautiful glossy, dark-green leaves, about 4 in (10 cm) long and 2 in (5 cm) wide. The waxy flowers, resembling roses in shape, vary in size from 2½ to 4 in (6 to 10 cm) across, in shades of pink and red. There are also white-flowered and white-streaked varieties.

CULTIVATION

If the plants you purchase are already in pots, they will probably not require potting on for at least two or three years, but if they are in containers you will need to transfer them to pots, preferably clay. Use the smallest size of pot which will comfortably hold the root-ball, which will probably be a 6 or 7-in (15 or 17.5-cm) pot. The main reason, in fact the only reason, for using a clay pot for camellias is that it is

Camellia japonica 'Adolphe Audusson'.

50

much heavier than a plastic pot, and some plants can become top-heavy if they are not balanced by the extra weight of a clay pot.

It is essential to provide a lime-free compost for camellias. They require the same type of compost used for rhododendrons and azaleas, which is:

One standard seed tray of peat.
One standard seed tray of leafmould.
One standard seed tray of sand.
To this mixture add:
3 oz (85 g) hoof and horn meal.
2 oz (56 g) bone meal.

If you are unable to obtain leafmould use garden loam (soil) or preferably loam from rotted-down turves. It is, of course, essential that any loam used is lime-free.

Camellias are not good plants for living room conditions because they prefer a temperature range, when flowering, of 45–60°F (7–15°C). The *Camellia japonica* varieties bloom during late winter and spring, depending on the particular variety grown. They are rather temperamental at this stage and any sudden change in conditions, when the buds are ready to open, is very likely to result in the buds dropping off the plants. Unlike azaleas they cannot be forced into flower by moving them to a warmer environment; they should be kept at the same temperature, ideally 50–55°F (10–13°C) during the day, while the flowers are opening and until the flowering period is over.

From the foregoing it will be appreciated that camellias are excellent plants for unheated conservatories and porches, and if they are placed in the position where they are to flower, a week or two before the buds open, you should not experience any bud drop. What you must avoid is sudden changes such as a low temperature to a high temperature; moist air conditions to dry air conditions. In other words the kind of change which would occur by transferring the plant from a cool greenhouse to a warm dry living-room atmosphere.

Watering the plants is no problem, unless you are in an area where the tap water is 'hard', in which case you should endeavour to use rainwater; but, in any case, if you water the plants with sequestrene in the spring and the autumn this will counteract the effects of the 'hard' water. The compost in the pots should be kept consistently moist throughout the growing season and never allowed to become too dry. After

Camellia japonica 'Mrs Tingley'. Camellias are ideal plants for porches or conservatories.

flowering the plants will not require watering as often because they have a resting period for a few weeks.

Any potting on which may become necessary should be carried out in late spring, and then the plants should be bedded out in the garden. Choose a situation where the plants are in partial shade. Dig a hole slightly deeper than the depth of the plant pot, and put a layer of peat at the bottom of the hole. Place the plant pot on the peat and fill the hole with soil, pressing down and round the pot to make sure it is firmly held in the ground. The rim of the pot should be about 1 in (2.5 cm) above ground level. Leave all the plants outside in this position until the end of the summer, then lift, clean the soil off the pots, and put them in the greenhouse.

Camellias can be fed during the summer months with any lime-free balanced liquid fertilizer. It is not necessary to feed plants during the season in which they have been potted on.

COLEUS
(Family Labiatae)

Coleus blumei hybrids are very easy-to-grow, brightly-coloured, foliage plants.

These plants are cultivated for the beauty of their leaves which occur in many different colours in considerable variety. The strains offered are all varieties of the parent species *Coleus blumei* which originates in Java. Coleus are perennials but are best treated as annuals, unless you wish to specialise in these plants and grow named varieties which can only be propagated by means of cuttings. They are difficult plants to overwinter because they are sensitive to cold and need a minimum temperature of 55°F (13°C). Cuttings root quite readily and are taken in the usual way from the ends of growing stems and inserted in any suitable cutting compost.

It is, however, the plants grown from seed with which we are concerned, and these are offered by seedsmen in several different mixtures or strains. Each strain has its own characteristic which may be shape of leaf, or predominance of colour, such as emphasis on yellow and green shades. A good mixture to start with is one which offers a wide range of colours, sometimes aptly described as a rainbow mixture.

CULTIVATION

Sow the seed during mid to late winter in soilless sowing compost or JI seed compost, and cover it with a thin layer of sand. Put the tray in a plastic bag or cover with a sheet of glass and place in the propagator at a temperature of 60 – 65°F (15 – 18°C). Germination takes about nine days, and as soon as the seedlings appear remove from the bag and put the seed pan in a good light to prevent the seedlings becoming drawn, which can easily occur at this stage.

As soon as some growth has been made it will probably be necessary to thin the seedlings; this is best done with a pair of tweezers. About four weeks after sowing the seedlings should be ready for transplanting, and at this stage you have to decide how many plants you wish to grow. Because there is such a variation in colouring in the coleus leaf there is also a considerable variation in attractiveness. It is impossible to see at the small seedling stage how the plant is going to develop and it is consequently necessary to grow the plant until the colours in the leaves can be seen.

By pricking out the seedlings into seed trays in a larger number than required, you can then select the best colours and discard the others. Also by this method you can get the widest variation because inevitably you get a considerable repetition in colour patterns.

Prick out about twice as many seedlings as the number you intend to grow. A standard seed tray will comfortably hold 36 plants. Use compost E6 or JI potting compost No.2.

Coleus are very pleasing plants to grow and are the ideal plant for the impatient gardener. They grow so quickly at the seedling stage that you can even see the daily growth and the amount of growth they make in a week is quite astonishing.

In three weeks the tiny seedlings you have pricked out in the seed tray will be showing the characteristics of how they are going to develop. You will then be in a position to make your selection, and to pot in 2½ to 3-in (6 to 7.5-cm) pots. In about four weeks the plants will be ready for their final potting in 4 or 4½-in (10-11.5 cm) pots. At all stages of potting use compost E6 or equivalent. You might read in some gardening manuals that coleus should be grown in lime-free soil, but in my experience the standard compost suitable for most plants gives excellent results which would not be bettered using a lime-free compost.

As growth proceeds from the seedling stage the plant will tend to grow a single stem, and as we are requiring a bushy plant bearing as many beautiful leaves as possible it is necessary to control the growth. As soon as four pairs of leaves have formed, take out the tiny tip of the growing point. This will cause new shoots to grow from the leaf axils; when these have made two pairs of leaves, again remove the growing tips.

The stopping of the plant in this way should produce a well-balanced bushy plant. After the second stop the plant will in due course begin to produce flower buds. These should be removed whenever they appear. Coleus usually remain very attractive until about the end of the summer (that is of course from a winter sowing), but then begin to deteriorate, and by the middle of autumn are ready for discarding.

CUPHEA
(Family Lythraceae)

Commonly known as the Mexican cigar flower, *Cuphea ignea* is an unusual plant which has a delicate charm. It flowers for a long period of time during the summer months, producing a continuous succession of flowers which are tubular, orange-scarlet in colour, about 1 in (2.5 cm) long, with ash-grey tips; the whole appearance is reminiscent of a miniature cigar. The plant will grow bushy if any straggly growth is checked, by pinching out the growing points, and, fully grown, is about 9 – 12 in (23 – 30 cm) high.

Cupheas can be grown from seed sown in spring, at a temperature of 65 – 70°F (18 – 21°C), when germination should take about 14 to 21 days. Alternatively, unless you are requiring a lot of plants, it is easier to purchase a well-grown plant and propagate as many plants as you require, the following spring.

CULTIVATION

Propagation, by cuttings, is carried out by selecting the strongest growing shoots and taking 2 – 2½-in (5 – 6-cm) long tip cuttings, severing the stem below a leaf node. Remove all but the top two pairs of leaves and insert the stem about ½ in (13 mm) deep in the rooting compost, after dipping the stem in a hormone rooting powder. Take cuttings in spring and keep enclosed under a plastic dome or a plastic bag until the cuttings can be left exposed without flagging. When the cuttings have rooted pot them in compost E6, or equivalent, in 3½-in (9-cm) pots and later in 4½ – 5-in (11.5 – 13-cm) pots as required.

Cupheas will survive in a normal living room temperature, in the summer months, and should be placed in a well-lit situation, as they benefit from direct sunshine.

Plants should be overwintered at 50 – 55°F (10 – 13°C) and will tolerate a temperature as low as 45°F (7°C).

Cuttings can be taken in summer, and the following year will produce larger plants earlier in the season than those obtained from spring cuttings. The difficulty of taking summer cuttings lies in overwintering the young plants which require a higher temperature than mature plants if they are to survive. It is better to raise a few new plants each year than to grow plants on for a second year.

Cuphea ignea is known as the Mexican Cigar Flower, because of the shape and appearance of its flower.

CYCLAMEN
(Family Primulaceae)

The greenhouse cyclamen of today is descended from the species *Cyclamen persicum* (syn. *C. latifolium*) which is found growing wild in Greece, Turkey, Syria, the Aegean Isles, Crete and Cyprus. The species has attractive heart-shaped marbled leaves and fragrant flowers which are small, the petals being narrow and twisted on quite long stems. The colour range is usually white, rose pink and various shades of lilac. There are no bright reds and crimsons. The species exhibits considerable variation in its foliage.

It was not until early in the nineteenth century that the cyclamen became popular as a pot plant in this country, but at this time the plants offered by nurserymen had flowers only slightly larger than the wild species.

During the first half of the nineteenth century new plants were brought into Great Britain in ever-increasing numbers and nurserymen and amateur growers were constantly striving to improve the species by cross-breeding and improving the growing conditions. It is not uncommon for cultivated plants which are constantly being interbred to develop new characteristics, and in 1870 a new race of cyclamen appeared which had large flowers. There does not seem to be any evidence that this change came about as a result of a breeding programme, and it has been suggested that intense cultivation, using the most suitable composts and ideal growing conditions, may have some bearing in the matter. A change of this kind is usually due to a mutation in the cell by an increase in the number of chromosomes or a change in the gene structure. Well-known examples of this are the Russell lupin and the Spencer sweet pea, and the results are, of course, very much improved forms almost overnight, as it were. This new development naturally stimulated the breeders and by 1875 plants had been produced which could be said to be the forerunners of the modern hybrids. At first only white and crimson shades were available but later a rose pink was raised.

In 1894 the nursery firm of Suttons introduced a salmon pink shade called 'Salmon Queen' and by crossing this with purple shades the brilliant crimsons were produced, but the flowers were rather small compared with today's plants.

This new race of large-flowered cyclamen had lost two of the desirable properties of the species, these being the fragrance of the flowers and the markings on the leaves; consequently efforts were made to restore these characteristics.

Breeders have more than succeeded with the leaf markings but with the search for fragrance the success has been much more limited, and up to the present time sweet-scented cyclamen hybrids do not compare in apprearance with the large-flowered non-fragrant hybrids either in size of flower or colour of petal.

In 1896 Vilmora introduced a strain possessing marbled leaves which he called 'Grandiflorum Zonale'. In Germany Meckel's 'Silber Blatt' (silver leaf) strain was introduced in 1904, but was by no means as ornamental as the modern silver leaf

Cyclamen persicum. If brought into flower by late autumn this plant will flower throughout the winter to the spring when kept in a cool situation.

varieties. In 1910 attempts were made to breed fragrant strains, and although some success was achieved the varieties did not become popular because the flowers lacked size and brilliance by comparison with the established hybrids, which still applies today, and so the search continues.

CULTIVATION

Cyclamen are grown from seed. The best times to sow are in mid-summer or mid-winter, depending on the facilities you have at your disposal. Cyclamen require a temperature range of 50–60°F (10–15°C) for continuous growth, which means an average temperature of 55°F (13°C). Moreover a moist environment is essential as the plants will not tolerate a dry atmosphere. If you can provide these conditions the best time to sow is in mid-summer, because it takes about 12 to 15 months to produce a really good plant. The alternative is to sow in winter, which means that by the time the seedlings are ready for potting it will be spring, and there will be no difficulty in providing good growing conditions.

You will not produce large plants by the winter, in fact some of the plants will not flower at all, and those that do will not compare with the summer-sown plant. You will however produce superb plants by the following autumn. An interesting feature of cyclamen is that its seed can be sown at almost any time of the year.

The seeds are large enough to handle and can therefore be sown separately 1 in (2.5 cm) apart (because the roots tend to spread out), and about ⅛–¼ in (3–6 mm) deep in either JI sowing compost or a soilless sowing compost.

The compost should be moist but not wet, because nowadays the practice is to put the seed pan (or pot) in a plastic bag which is then sealed to prevent any loss of moisture.

If the compost is too wet the seeds will rot. A minimum temperature of 60°F (15°C) is required for germination, and if this is maintained the first seedlings should appear in four to five weeks. The seed pan should then be taken out of the plastic bag and covered with a sheet of glass during the day and removed at night. It is not essential to cover with glass, but you must ensure that the surface of the compost does not dry out while the roots are still small. To have to water the pots at this stage is not desirable because if there is too much dampness the seedlings can rot. The first growth to appear is a single leaf. In due course a second leaf appears, by which time the seedlings are ready for potting in 2½-in (6-cm) pots. Germination is usually somewhat erratic; moreover you cannot expect 100 per cent germination, it will more probably be 60–80 per cent.

When seeds are sown in mid-summer germination is usually complete after about two months, but naturally this period will be somewhat longer with winter sowing.

The seedlings must be lifted with care from seed pans because the roots are easily broken. It will be seen that a tiny corm has developed, and this should be placed just below the surface when potting in the first 2½-in (6-cm) pots.

It is essential for the production of a first-class plant to maintain steady continuous growth, without any checks from the time of sowing until flowering, and this is particularly true of the cyclamen.

Strive therefore to give your plants the ideal conditions they require, which in the case of cyclamen is about 55–60°F (12–15°C), a humid atmosphere and bright light but not direct sunlight. In the winter months the light intensity is often below the requirements for growth, and at such times the plants cease to grow, but if you are able to provide artificial light for nine or ten hours a day and a minimum day temperature of 50°F (10°C) growth will continue. Cyclamen are very responsive to artificial light and any plants which are developing late can be brought into flower by early winter, which would otherwise remain in bud until late winter. A suitable source of light is a warm white fluorescent tube suspended about 18 in (45 cm) above the plants.

When the 2½-in (6-cm) pots are well rooted pot on into 3½-in (9-cm) pots and later into 5-in (13-cm) pots. The compost to use for cyclamen can be either a soilless type or John Innes type, but it is important to ensure that it is free from lime and on the acid side, having a pH 6 to 6.5, also that it is an open compost which will drain easily. It is generally agreed by the specialist growers that it is not desirable to use sterilised soil for growing cyclamen, but why this should be is not explained. A rich compost is desirable, such as potting compost E2.

When potting into 3½-in (9-cm) pots, the corm should be positioned slightly above the surface of the compost and for the final potting in 5-in (13-cm) pots the corm should have about one third above the surface.

A well-grown cyclamen has a considerable number of leaf stems and flower stems growing out of the top of the corm and should water lodge in this area the corm is liable to rot. By having the corm above the surface of the compost, the chances of this happening at the time of watering are considerably lessened.

It is often recommended that cyclamen should be watered from the bottom by standing the pot in water, thus ensuring that there is no chance of water spilling onto the plant, but this method of watering has the drawback that it leaches the soluble salts out of the compost, and when the excess water runs out of the pot it carries with it valuable soluble salts. If the plant is constantly watered by this method it will not be long before the plant is short of nutrients, particularly potash which is usually present in the compost in the form of sulphate of potash, which is a water-soluble salt.

The best method is to water the plant by pointing the spout towards the side of the pot and not allowing the water level to rise above the top of the corm.

When the plants have finished flowering, the time has come to cease watering to allow the compost to dry. Cyclamen are usually allowed a short resting period during which time the leaves slowly die off and you are left with a dry corm. It is not essential completely to dry off the plants and they can be kept growing with the compost kept fairly dry, but in an active greenhouse it is more convenient to put them under the bench and leave more room for the spring and summer plants, which will already be requiring all the room you have available.

It is usually recommended that growth should be restarted in summer but in my experience this does not leave enough growing time to get the plants into bloom by early winter. If you fail to do this the growth during winter is very slow.

Most amateurs cannot afford to provide a greenhouse temperature of 55°F (13°C) during these months, and unless you provide ideal growing conditions during the winter months a summer start will result in your plants remaining in bud until late winter or early spring. On the other hand if you can bring the plants into bloom by early winter, this slowness of growth is an advantage, because the blooms last for weeks on end and the plants will give a good show for over four months.

By starting the plants into growth in early summer it is not difficult to achieve this. Knock the old corms out of their pots and remove all the old compost and dead roots. Repot in fresh compost with the corm about one third above the level of the compost, and water until the compost is moist, then place in a lightly shaded frame or outside in a good light position, but not a sunny spot. Leave the pots outside until early autumn, then take them into the greenhouse by which time they should be in good leaf with flower buds showing.

Plants grown from seed sown in summer are, of course, kept growing continuously until after they flower the following autumn or winter, and the same applies to winter sowings. They should be kept in the greenhouse until the early summer then put outside, sheltered from the direct rays of the sun, or in a shaded frame. In late summer put the plants back in the greenhouse.

EXACUM
(Family Gentianaceae)

Exacum affine flowers for two or three months in the summer.

The species *Exacum affine* was only introduced to Europe at the beginning of the twentieth century. It was found growing on the island of Socotra, which is situated at the entrance of the Gulf of Aden. The cultivar *Exacum affine* 'Midget' is the variety usually offered for sale by seedsmen, and it is a more compact plant than the species, growing to about 9 in (23 cm) in height. The plants are naturally bushy, and when in flower are covered all over with small fragrant mauve or lavender-blue flowers, with a cluster of golden anthers in the centre. The flowers are saucer-shaped and usually ¼ – ½ in (6 – 13 mm) across.

Plants are freely available and should be bought when the first flowers are beginning to open; they should then give a continuity of bloom for two or three months. However, exacums are very easy to grow from seed and if you require several plants it is more economical to grow your own.

CULTIVATION

Sow the small seeds on the surface of a soilless seed compost and gently tap the pot to settle the seeds into the compost. Then lightly dampen the surface of the compost with a fine spray of water and cover the seed pan with a sheet of glass. Place in a temperature of 60–65°F (15–18°C) and keep covered until germination is evident, then remove the glass and place in a good light, protected from direct sunlight. When the seedlings are large enough to handle, pot in 2½-in (6-cm) pots, in compost E6, and finally in 4 or 4½-in (10 or 11.5-cm) pots, depending on the growth the plant has made.

To make steady growth the plants require a temperature of 60–65°F (15–18°C) and although seed can be sown from late winter to spring, in order to obtain flowering plants the same year it is not advisable to sow earlier than early spring, unless you are able to provide the temperature requirement. Of course, the earlier the seeds are sown, the earlier the plants will bloom and the longer the flowering period, in fact, if seed is sown in summer the plant will bloom the following summer, but you would have to maintain a minimum temperature of 50–55°F (10–13°C) throughout the winter, and even so you would probably lose a few plants. Seed sown in early spring should produce flowering plants by the middle of summer.

When plants are in bloom, never allow the compost to become too dry, otherwise the flowers will shrivel up and die. As the flowers fade they should be removed to ensure continuity of flowering. Although exacums are perennials they should be treated as greenhouse annuals and discarded after flowering. When a good compost, such as E6, is used, it is not necessary to feed the plants during their short growing season; otherwise start feeding about eight to ten weeks after their final potting.

FUCHSIA
(Family Onagraceae)

Charles Plumier is recorded as finding the first fuchsias in 1703 in San Domingo in the West Indies, which he named *Fuchsia tryphylla flore coccinea*. The name *Fuchsia* was in commemoration of Leonhart Fuchs, (1501–66), a physician and herbalist. Father Charles Plumier, or Pere Plumier, was a

distinguished French traveller and botanist, who made three voyages to the West Indies and tropical South America, and in 1703 he published a book dealing with the plants he had discovered in his travels, including the fuchsia he had found.

Half a century later Linnaeus re-named it *Fuchsia tryphylla*, as it is known today. As the years passed, further species were found and added to the genus, but *Fuchsia tryphylla* was not amongst them and for over 150 years it was not seen again. In 1873 Thomas Hogg of New York received some seeds from the West Indies and some nine years later one of the resultant plants came into the hands of Messrs Henderson & Sons, the London fuchsia specialists at that time, who sent it to Kew for identification. It was found to be the long lost *Fuchsia tryphylla*.

The first fuchsia introduced to Great Britain was in

this story say it was her husband). However, terms were agreed; here again versions vary, as some say James Lee gave her all the money in his pocket, about eight guineas, and others that he came back the next day and kept increasing his offer until she finally accepted a price of eighty guineas, but this latter version would appear less likely. One thing is certain and that is that she would not part with it until he agreed to let her have the first two cuttings. By 1790 James Lee had raised 300 plants from the original fuchsia, and these he sold for one guinea each. It is not recorded which species it was.

The first known record of a hybrid was in 1832, being a cross between *F. coccinea* and *F. magellanica*, after which many hybrids were raised. Towards the end of the nineteenth century there were 1,500 or so named varieties, but, like many plants, hundreds of these were lost during the two world wars, and nowadays it is doubtful if a third of these old varieties still exist, despite the fact that varieties have kept turning up, from many amateur growers, which have been passed on from one grower to another. As with all groups of popular plants, such as pelargoniums and chrysanthemums, many new varieties have been bred during the past thirty years, and the modern hybrids are usually superior to the old ones.

There are two main groups of fuchsias: hardy fuchsias, which are grown as permanent bushes in the garden, and greenhouse fuchsias which are grown in pots and need protection in the colder months, as they are not frost-hardy. As we are only dealing with greenhouse and house plants, it is the cultivation of the latter group which is described.

1788, by a Captain Firth, who presented it to the Botanical Gardens at Kew. It is not certain whether this was the species *F. coccinea*, or *F. macrostemma*. The first fuchsias offered commercially were probably by Mr James Lee, a famous nurseryman of Hammersmith in the eighteenth and early nineteenth centuries.

It would seem that James Lee was informed by one of his customers that they had seen a very pretty and unusual plant in the window of a cottage in Wapping. His curiosity aroused, he went to see for himself and when he saw the plant he quickly realised the commercial value, and was consequently keen to acquire it. The woman who owned it was, however, reluctant to part with it because it had a sentimental value for her, having been brought home to her from South America by her sailor son (some versions of

CULTIVATION

Although fuchsias can be grown quite easily from seeds, it is more satisfactory to grow named varieties which are superior and have the advantage of enabling you to select the flowers which most appeal to you. There are a number of specialist growers and also many nurserymen who offer a selection; consequently, it is easy to obtain the varieties of your choice.

The best time to purchase plants is in the spring, and the only attention these will require is pruning or stopping as the shoots grow. Assuming the plant has two or three growths, these should be stopped above the second pair of leaves; and when the new shoots, which grow from the leaf axils, have produced two pairs of leaves pinch out the growing tips. The purpose is to produce a bushy plant with numerous shoots, and after each stop two new growths should appear from the dormant buds on each side of the stem. Starting with three shoots, the first stop should produce six new growths, and after the second stop there should be twelve.

Unfortunately plants do not always behave as they should, which is one of their attractions; nevertheless two stops will usually suffice to produce a satisfactory plant. Unless it is already in a 4½-in (11.5-cm) pot when you buy it, you will need to pot on into this size or into a 5-in (12.5-cm) pot as the plant makes growth. Use compost E6 or JI No.2.

When the plants have finished flowering, withhold water, and allow the compost to dry out, but not to become bone dry. Keep the plants in the cool part of the greenhouse and gradually they will shed all their leaves. When stored with a dry compost and completely dormant the plants only require a frost-free temperature and will not suffer any damage even if the greenhouse temperature drops to 32°F (0°C).

In late winter the plants can be started into growth providing you can accommodate them in a slightly warmer temperature, minimum 40°F (4°C). After the first year's growth has been completed, you will notice that the main stem and most of the side shoots have become rigid and woody. Growth is started by watering the plants. It is not necessary to soak the pots, just water with a watering can up to the brim of the pot, twice in succession, and if you find that the compost feels dry in two or three days' time water them again. From then on only water when necessary. After watering prune the plants by cutting out any weak growths and shortening all the side shoots back to two nodes, cutting just above the node. In a short time you will notice green shoots growing from the nodes on the stems, and that is the time to repot the plants.

Remove the plants from the pots and remove the old compost from the roots, as described in the cultivation of pelargoniums. The plants are then repotted into the same size of pot, using compost E6, and later, when new roots have filled the pot, they should be potted on into the next size of pot.

Before this move is required the new shoots will have made considerable growth, and each growth is stopped after two pairs of leaves, unless you wish to take cuttings. It is better to take cuttings in the spring, because autumn cuttings have to be kept growing through the winter, and this requires heat which is an unnecessary expense. Once you have a collection of plants the sole purpose of taking cuttings is to keep a succession of young plants to replace the three-year-old plants, which should be discarded, as a general rule.

After three years, bush-grown fuchsias are usually too big for growing in pots and, apart from other considerations, take up too much room in the greenhouse.

For cuttings, allow the shoots to make four pairs of leaves, and when the fifth pair is just visible cut the shoot below the node on which the bottom pair are growing. After you have removed the bottom two pairs of leaves, this will give you a cutting with two pairs of leaves and the growing tip. Insert the cuttings into a suitable cutting compost, enclosing the container in a polythene bag or cover with a plastic dome, to maintain a moist atmosphere until root growth commences. As soon as the cuttings are obviously growing, pot into 3½-in (9-cm) pots in compost E6 or similar, and after six pairs of leaves have formed take out the growing tip, then proceed as described for bush plants.

STANDARDS AND HALF STANDARDS

Fuchsias are excellent plants to grow as standards, as this method of culture shows off the flowers to perfection. The procedure is to confine the growth to a single stem until it has reached the required height, which in the case of a standard is 30 in (75 cm) from the soil level to the first side shoot, and for half-standards 18 – 20 in (45 – 50 cm).

For this purpose the cutting, which is a single stem, is not stopped, but instead any side shoots which develop in the leaf axils are immediately removed, but the leaves themselves must be allowed to remain. When the desired height has been reached grow on for at least another six to eight pairs of leaves, then remove the growing tip. The stem will need supporting with a cane as it grows, because it is essential that it grows straight. Ensure that the cane is close to the stem.

It is not necessary to use a 2-ft (60-cm) or 3-ft (90-cm) cane while the cutting plant is in the 3½-in (9-cm) pot, as this would be a bit top heavy, so use a thin, suitable size at first, and replace it when necessary or when potting on into a 5-in (12.5-cm) pot. The effect of removing the tip of the plant is that side shoots appear in the leaf axils of the top six to eight pairs of leaves.

Allow each side shoot to form three pairs of leaves, then pinch out the top and repeat the process with the new side shoots. Two stops will be sufficient, and be flexible with the stopping, as some shoots grow longer than others. Endeavour to produce a well-balanced head on the plant, bearing in mind that the growth of the side shoots, or laterals as they are called, is cruciform, so you can foresee which way the new shoots will grow. It will be appreciated that stopping the growth of shoots by nipping off the tip will delay flowering, which it does by about six weeks. All stopping should ideally be completed before early summer, to obtain a full season's flowering. When the standards have produced a fair amount of growth at the top, all the leaves on the main stem, up to the first shoots, should be removed as they are no longer required. Standards and half-standards can be kept usefully for more than three years because it takes two years to produce a good

Gloxinias in the greenhouse. Gloxinia is the popular name for *Sinningia speciosa* hybrids, which are available in an extensive range of colours.

'head' on the plant and each year it can be severely pruned to keep a well-balanced appearance. On the greenhouse bench it only takes up a minimum of bench space because the foliage is well above the height of most other plants.

There are many different varieties of hybrids of fuchsias and new names are constantly being introduced. Most hybrids make good bush grown plants, but not all are suitable for growing as standards. It depends on the type of growth the plant produces. 'Tennessee Waltz' makes a very fine standard, because it has thin stems which arch, whereas 'Ballet Girl' has much thicker stems which are more rigid and it does not usually produce a good standard plant. It is advisable, therefore, to try different varieties to find the ones which are the most suitable for the type of plant you wish to grow.

GLOXINIA – SINNINGIA
(Family Gesneriaceae)

William Lobb, a plant collector employed by the famous Veitch Nurseries, introduced the first gloxinia to England. The correct Latin name for the species is *Sinningia*, named after a German horticulturist W. Sinning (1794 – 1874) who was the Curator of the Botanical Garden in Bonn. *Sinningia speciosa*, which comes from Brazil, is the main parent from which today's hybrids were developed. It has purple blue

flowers which droop, and it was not until the mid-nineteenth century that upright flowers were produced. The name commonly used by gardeners for this plant is *Gloxinia*, after Benjamin Peter Gloxin, a physician and botanist of Strasbourg, about 1785.

CULTIVATION

Gloxinias can be grown from seed or tubers but to start a small collection it is better to buy tubers which are usually offered as named varieties and, by and large, are superior to the plants you are likely to raise from seed.

The tubers you can buy are usually one year old and are about $1\frac{1}{4} - 1\frac{1}{2}$ in ($32 - 38$ mm) in diameter. A perfectly-formed tuber is round underneath and slightly concave at the top and this is your guide for planting because it is, of course, important to plant the tuber the right way up. Sometimes tubers are almost spherical and it is very difficult to determine which is the underside. Should you unfortunately pot the tuber the wrong way up the shoots will commence growing first and there will not be any root growth; consequently, if most of the tubers are showing short growth, and one or two are not, remove the apparently dormant tubers and examine them for growth. If tiny yellowish green growth has taken place you will know that you have planted them upside down, so turn them over and no harm will have been done.

Gloxinias need a fairly rich compost which should be on the acid side, pH 6, such as compost E3. Using 5-in (12.5-cm) pots, fill up to the brim, press the tuber into the compost until the top is about $\frac{1}{2}$ in (13 mm) below the rim of the pot, then press the compost down all round the tuber until it is firm. Put more compost in the pot until it is just below the level of the top of the tuber, which should always be just above the surface, thus ensuring that it is always exposed to the air. This prevents the tuber from remaining in a wet state which could cause it to rot.

After the potting has been completed, fill the pots up to the brim with water and place in the propagator, temperature $60 - 70°F$ ($15 - 21°C$).

It is necessary to prevent the compost from becoming too dry, but on the other hand it is detrimental to overwater at this stage, before root growth is well under way, as this would cause the tubers to rot.

No further attention is required other than moderate watering until the shoot growths are about $\frac{1}{2} - 1$ in ($13 - 25$ mm) long, when you should select the strongest shoot and remove all the others. Confining growth to one shoot in this way gives you a well-shaped plant and larger flowers.

The time to plant your tubers is determined by the heat you can provide, because gloxinias need day temperatures from $60°F$ ($15°C$) upwards and a minimum of $50°F$ ($10°C$) by night.

By the middle of spring, the day temperatures inside the greenhouse are usually satisfactory for gloxinias and, providing heat is available when needed on any cold nights, gloxinias will be happy on the greenhouse benches.

You can start gloxinias any time from mid-winter onwards but bearing in mind that it will be necessary to keep them in the propagator until mid-spring it is usually more practical to start potting in early spring. Unless you wish to have your plants all in bloom at the same time it is better to pot them in batches at intervals of two to three weeks; this will result in plants flowering in succession over a longer period.

Starting the tubers into growth in spring, the plants should be in flower through the summer, and by the autumn you should cease watering and allow the compost to dry out.

Tubers can be stored either by leaving them in the pots or by removing them from the compost and storing in a cool but not too cold place in the house. If left in the pots under a bench in the greenhouse they will survive night temperatures down to $42°F$ ($6°C$) providing the compost is dust-dry, but if it is even slightly damp they are liable to rot.

Tubers can be grown year after year, and each year they increase in size requiring larger pots. Three-year-old tubers will usually require a 6-in (15-cm) pot. A good guide to the size of pot required is to allow about 1 in (2.5 cm) of space between the tuber and the side of the pot.

Gloxinias can easily be raised from seed which germinates quite freely. Sow in soilless sowing compost or JI sowing compost in mid-summer or mid-winter. Cover the seed lightly, place the seed pan in a plastic bag and put in a temperature of $65 - 70°F$ ($18 - 21°C$). When the seedlings are large enough to handle prick out into a seed tray using compost E3.

The seedlings need to be kept growing in a temperature of about $65°F$ ($18°C$), and this means

Gloxinia 'Emperor Frederik'.

that they need the accommodation of the propagator, thus by pricking out into seed trays precious room is saved at a time when the propagator is needed for many other plants. Gloxinias transplant very well, if done carefully, with hardly any check in growth. When the plants are about 1 – 1½ in (25 – 38 mm) in diameter, transplant into 3½-in (9 – cm) pots in compost E3, and those plants which grow large enough can be potted on into 4½-in (11.5 – cm) pots. Seeds sown in winter usually flower by autumn, and those sown in summer flower by the following summer and do, of course, build up bigger tubers by the end of the season. Unless you are able to provide a high enough temperature throughout the winter months it is obviously better to sow in winter. After flowering the plants should be allowed to dry out in the same way as the tuber-grown plants.

Gloxinias grown from seed show a wide range of colours, and although it takes longer to produce large plants than by starting with tubers it is a much more economical way of building up a collection.

Gloxinias can be propagated by whole leaf cuttings.

Gloxinia 'Violacea'.

Select a young leaf in early summer and break it off, making sure that the whole stem is intact. Half fill a 4½-in (11.5-cm) pot with soilless cutting compost and, after dipping the stem in a hormone rooting compound, push it into the compost to a depth of ½ in (13 mm). A pot of this size will hold three leaf cuttings. Place a polythene bag over the cuttings, securing the open end of the bag to the pot by means of a rubber band or string. The cutting compost should be moist but not wet, and the cuttings need to be kept enclosed until roots have formed at the base of

the stem. Examine the cuttings regularly to check whether the leaves are showing any signs of rotting. Remove any part of the leaf which is not healthy, or even the whole cutting if necessary, otherwise it will contaminate the healthy cuttings. When the cuttings have grown roots, pot in compost E6 supporting the original leaf if necessary, and when new leaves have grown the old leaf should be cut off the new plant.

Fig. 5 Gloxinia leaf cuttings. (a) Select young leaves about 3–4 in (7–10 cm) long, complete with the full length of leaf stem. (b) Dip the stem in hormone rooting powder and insert the full length of the stem into the rooting compost. (c) Cover with a plastic dome for several weeks until roots have formed.

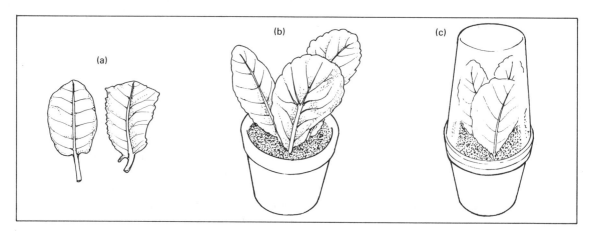

HYDRANGEA
(Family Hydrangeaceae; formerly Saxifragaceae)

The common hydrangea with its large mop head, so often seen growing in parks and gardens and offered by florists as a pot plant, is of hybrid origin, mainly derived from *Hydrangea macrophylla*, which is a species of Japanese origin. There are two types of hybrids in the group, namely lace caps and hortensia hybrids.

The variety known as 'Blue Wave' is a good example of the Lace Caps, which have dense heads with only a few outer florets showing the petals. The hortensia types have large round heads of sterile flowers with large petals which are fully open over the whole flower head.

Nurserymen usually force hydrangeas into flower in the spring and this is the best time to buy plants, which are usually available with flowers in shades of pink, red, white and blue. The pink-flowered varieties range from light pink to deep rose; and these can be changed into blue flowers by treating the soil with a hydrangea 'blueing compound' or aluminium sulphate. The lighter shades of pinks convert to the most attractive shades of blue. Only pinks can be changed to blue, because reds turn a mauvy-purple. It is apparently the absorption of aluminium by the plant which changes the colour from pink to blue; and when the soil is neutral or has a good lime content this seems to prevent the assimilation of aluminium by the plant. Consequently, in order to keep pink shades pure in shade the compost should have a good chalk or lime content. White flowers are unaffected by the acidity or alkalinity of the soil.

CULTIVATION
When the hydrangea you have purchased in the spring has finished flowering it should, by that time,

Hydrangea macrophylla 'Hortensia', grown in alkaline soil.

have produced some basal growths. In this case, cut out the old flowering branches. If there are no basal shoots apparent, severely prune the flowering branches and wait for new shoots to appear. When pruning always cut the shoot just above a node.

Hydrangeas do not require much heat at any time and plants should be put outside in the full sun as soon as flowering is over and kept growing in the best possible conditions, because the next season's flowers depend on the development of the plant at this time. You may have noticed that after a good summer the hydrangeas in the garden are a mass of flowers the following year, whereas after a cold wet summer the next year the flowers are few and far between.

Hydrangeas are gross feeders and also require to be kept well-watered. Feed the plant every 14 days until the end of the summer and then reduce the watering. Ideally, plants should be exposed to cold conditions in autumn in order to chill the plants, which causes the leaves to drop. It is important, however, not to expose plants in pots to frost as damage could result. A temperature of 35–45°F (2–7°C) for a night or two should cause the leaf fall.

Hydrangea macrophylla 'Hortensia' hybrid is an attractive pot plant and can be planted in the garden when it grows too large for its pot. This is the colour produced by acid soil.

When the plants have shed all their leaves, watering for the dormant period should be kept to a minimum, just sufficient to prevent the compost from becoming dry.

In winter, depending how early you wish your plants to bloom, repot the plants in fresh compost using JI No.3 after removing the old compost from the roots with as little damage to the roots as possible. This is best done while the compost in the pots is dry.

After repotting in the same size of pot, or a size larger if necessary, the plants should be watered and placed in a temperature averaging about 50°F (10°C), until they show some sign of growth, when the temperature should be increased to 55–60°F (13–15°C). Keep the plants well watered, and in the case of blue-flowered plants treat with 'blueing compound' as soon as flowering buds start to show. If no buds are seen after four pairs of leaves, the shoot is not likely to develop a flower bud.

Propagation of hydrangeas is by cuttings, which are best taken in spring. Select a flowerless shoot and cut below the third or fourth node from the tip. Ideally cuttings should be about 3 or 4 in (7.5 or 10 cm) long. Remove all the leaves except the top one or two pairs, and insert about 1 in (2.5 cm) deep in soilless cutting compost. A hormone rooting powder helps. The cuttings need to be kept in a moist atmosphere until some roots have formed, as the leaves soon flag, so the pots need to be enclosed in a polythene or plastic bag for some seven to ten days. Cuttings take from three to six weeks to root, depending on the growing conditions, after which they should be potted in 3½-in (9-cm) pots in JI No.3 and kept growing steadily through the summer.

New plants can be treated in two ways. The plant can be grown as a single shoot with the object of producing one large bloom the following year, or alternatively it can be made to bush by the process of stopping. If a bushy plant is required, stop the shoot above the second or third pair of leaves. When new shoots appear, four are sufficient, but if there are fewer a further stop will be necessary. All stopping must be completed in mid-summer or there is not time for the flower buds to form and ripen for the following season's flowers.

IMPATIENS
(Family Balsaminaceae)

Known much more widely by its common name 'Busy Lizzie', this plant has become very popular in the last 20 years and possibly now rivals the geranium as a window-ledge plant. It is not a difficult plant to grow and has the virtue that, given the right conditions, it will bloom almost the whole year round.

The seeds and plants available today are cultivars, which have been developed by hybridising the species *Impatiens holsti*, *I. sultani* and *I. petersiana*. The cultivated Busy Lizzie has been given the specific name *Impatiens wallerana*. Thus we have *I.W. sultani*, from which the cultivars with pale green leaves have been produced; *I.W. petersiana*, giving the cultivars with purplish bronze leaves and red stems; and *I.W. sultani variegata* giving plants with white-edged leaves and candy-striped flowers.

The species are native to Zanzibar and also to tropical East Africa. A comparatively recent

Impatiens wallerana, better known as Busy Lizzie, flowers throughout the year.

development has been the introduction of plants from New Guinea, from which cultivars with variegated foliage and larger flowers have been raised.

The Busy Lizzies sold today are mostly cultivars which have a compact bushy growth and a colour range of various shades of red, pink, orange and also a white; in addition there are the striped bicolours, such as red striped with white.

CULTIVATION

The best way to start with a collection of impatiens is to buy the plants and propagate from cuttings, which can be taken at any time of the year. A good time to take cuttings is in the late summer, when the plants are growing strongly, and also because the purpose of taking cuttings is to provide plants for the following season.

Select the most suitable stems and take tip cuttings about 2–3 in (5–7.5 cm) long, cutting the stem below a node, dust with a rooting powder and insert the cutting about ½ in (13 mm) deep into a cutting compost. A lot of people root Busy Lizzies by standing the cutting in water but, although roots form quite readily by this method, they are always thin and weak with the result that the cuttings do not always survive after being potted in the compost.

Cuttings taken in a mixture of 60 parts soilless cutting compost to 40 parts fine vermiculite produce a much healthier and bushier root system.

Keep the cuttings covered by a plastic bag, or by similar means, until they are growing away; and when they are well rooted pot in compost E6, in 3½-in (9-cm) pots. At this stage the plants need to be watered very carefully to avoid any possibility of the stems rotting. Busy Lizzies have rather soft succulent stems, which will rot if kept too wet, so, after potting the cutting, water once and then allow the compost just to surface dry before watering again. The frequency of watering will, of course, depend on the weather, but it is essential that the plants are not overwatered at this stage. It is a good idea to take more cuttings than you need, until you become experienced in growing these plants, and you can then afford a few losses. If you do not have any losses

no doubt your friends will be only too pleased to take your surplus plants off your hands.

Busy Lizzies grow well in a temperature range of 60–70°F (15–20°C) which is easily maintained in the summer months. In the early spring and late autumn try to maintain a minimum temperature of 60°F (15°C), as below this plants will cease to grow satisfactorily and will cease flowering. Below 55°F (13°C) the plant will tend to lose its leaves, and if the compost is too wet the stems are likely to rot.

When the plant in a 3½-in (9-cm) pot has made good growth, and looks ready for potting on, examine the root system and do not pot on unless it is almost

Double-flowered *Impatiens*. This variety of Busy Lizzie is an easy-to-grow attractive pot plant.

pot-bound. Like many plants the Busy Lizzie flowers more prolifically when the pot is full of roots, and potting on too soon is one of the causes of poor flowering.

Having examined the plant in its 3½-in (9-cm) pot, and found it to be full of roots, pot on into a 4½ or 5-in (11.5 or 13-cm) pot, again using compost E6. It is not usually necessary to use a larger pot than a 5-in (13-cm) even for the biggest plants.

If cuttings are taken in summer, the young plants can be overwintered in their 3½-in (9-cm) pots and will be ready for potting on into larger pots in the spring. When compost E6 is used it will not be necessary to feed the plants until late summer, if at all. On the other hand, if you use a soilless compost, feeding should commence about six to eight weeks after the plants have been potted into their final pots.

Always endeavour to prevent any spindly growth and give the plants regular attention, pinching out any growths as necessary, to produce a bushy plant. Busy Lizzies are not difficult plants to keep alive, once they are established plants, but if you wish to grow really attractive plants they do require cultivating in the manner described.

Poor flowering and loss of flowers can be caused by too little light. Loss of leaves is often caused by

irregular watering in the summer, and by insufficient heat in the colder seasons of the year. In hot weather the plants will require more water than most pot plants and will probably need watering at least once a day.

Impatiens can be raised quite easily from seed if you have the facilities. Sow in late winter or early spring, in a seed compost, covering the seeds very lightly with the compost. Keep the seed pan in a plastic bag in a temperature of 65–70°F (18–21°C), and germination should take place in two to three weeks. Remove the plastic bag as soon as germination is evident and put the seed pan in slightly cooler conditions, 60–65°F (15–18°C), in a good light but protected from direct sunlight. When the seedlings have made some growth and are large enough to handle, they can be potted in 2½-in (6-cm) pots using compost E6.

In the right conditions growth is quite rapid and seeds sown in late winter will usually give flowering plants by mid-summer.

The usual procedure with impatiens is to discard plants after a full season's growth but, should you wish to keep the plant, it should be severely cut back in autumn and it will shoot again from the base, in much the same manner as a geranium does. If you decide to do this the plant should be repotted in the spring in fresh compost, removing as much of the old compost as possible.

KALANCHOE
(Family Crassulaceae)

This plant has become very popular in recent years, largely because it is possible to induce it to bloom for most of the year.

Kalanchoes are short-day plants, which means that they will only flower when they have experienced a period of short days. Their natural time for blooming is from mid-winter to mid-spring, but, if their exposure to daylight is restricted to a maximum of ten hours daylight with fourteen hours darkness in each twenty-four hour period, in about two to three months they will come into bloom.

There is not much point in inducing kalanchoes to flower during the summer months, but they are very useful for the autumn and early winter when flowering pot plants are scarce.

To induce flowering during this period, plants should be restricted to eight to ten hours daylight in each calendar day by covering the plants with black paper or any material which ensures that the plants are in complete darkness. Three months after this treatment begins the plants should commence blooming, so if you wish to have plants in bloom at the beginning of autumn you commence covering the plants in mid-summer.

Chrysanthemums are another example of short-day plants, and this is why nurserymen are able to offer them in flower, in pots, the whole year round.

Kalanchoes are most useful plants because not only are the flowers bright shades of red, and there is also a bright yellow, but they are also very good house plants; in fact, they are undemanding plants and if you forget to water them no harm will be done as they will stand periods of drought.

The genus includes several species of flowering plants and also plants with decorative foliage, but it is the dwarf species *Kalanchoe blossfeldiana*, a compact plant with bright red flowers, growing to about 12 in (30 cm) in height, and the smaller variety *Kalanchoe* 'Vulcan', about 9 in (23 cm), with which we are concerned. The variety or cultivar 'Vulcan' is obtainable with bright red or bright yellow flowers. There are other cultivars similar to *K.* 'Vulcan'.

The plants have thick fleshy green leaves which are often tinged with red round the edges. They have a long blooming period of some two to three months. This long flowering period, and the fact that they are such good house plants, makes them suitable for decorative bowls of mixed house plants.

CULTIVATION
Kalanchoes are grown from seed and can be raised quite easily; and should you wish to retain a particular plant it is possible to take cuttings, which are not particularly difficult to root.

Sow seed in spring in any type of sowing compost, covering the seed very lightly, in a temperature of 60–65°F (15–18°C) and enclose in a plastic bag or cover the seed pan with a sheet of glass, and remove these coverings at the first signs of germination. As soon as the seedlings are large enough to handle, pot in 2½-in (6-cm) pots; they are slow-growing plants and this size of pot will probably suffice until the end of the summer or even the following spring. Dwarf varieties never require more than a 3½-in (9-cm) pot and will grow for two years in this size, after which it is usually better to discard them.

Cuttings can be taken during the summer months. If left in the cutting medium for six to seven weeks, they should be well rooted and ready for potting in 2½-in (6-cm) pots.

Kalanchoe blossfeldiana is an ideal window-ledge plant which remains in bloom for a long period.

For cuttings, select strong shoots about 2 in (5 cm) long, and cut below a node. Remove all the leaves except the top five, and, after dipping in a hormone rooting powder, insert about ½ in (13 mm) deep in a cutting compost. Keep the cuttings enclosed inside a plastic dome or a plastic bag for about three weeks and then expose them to the air for another three or four weeks before potting.

Kalanchoes tend to grow a single stem, and to obtain bushy plants it is necessary to stop the growth by removing the tip of the stem. This should not be done until the cuttings have made at least 1 in (2.5 cm) of growth. Side shoots will appear in due course, and when these have made sufficient growth remove the growing points of these as well.

If you only wish to grow a few kalanchoes it is probably better to buy the plants and propagate your requirements by cuttings, which are very easily raised, rather than grow them from seed, particularly as it takes about eighteen months to grow a good flowering plant.

Kalanchoes require a minimum temperature of 45°F (7°C) during the winter but they will not thrive if kept at this temperature. To make satisfactory growth they require a temperature of 60–65°F (15–18°C); consequently they need to be kept in a propagator in the greenhouse if they are to flower satisfactorily during the winter months. Once they have been brought into flower they can be put in a cooler temperature to retard growth and prolong the flowering period.

LANTANA
(Family Verbenaceae)

The species are mainly of South American origin and are of interest only as the parents of the hybrid varieties which are vastly superior. The principal species used in raising the hybrids were *Lantana camara* which occurs with yellow, red or violet flowers, *L. nivea* (white) and *L. trifolia* (red). *L. camara* grows wild on all the islands of the Dutch East Indies, as well as tropical South America, where infusion from the leaves is used as a tonic and a stimulant. It has the common name Surinam tea plant. Lantanas are half-hardy evergreen shrubby plants and in warm countries are often used as hedges. In the 1960s there was a lantana hedge round the swimming pool of the Nile Hilton Hotel in Cairo, which may still be there, and lantanas were also used as a screen round the garden of a cafe at the foot of the Acropolis in Athens.

The species already mentioned are upright in growth and bloom in the summer months, but there is another species, *L. sellowiana*, which has a trailing habit. It has lilac flowers and is more likely to bloom in the winter. At one time there were many named varieties of lantana such as 'Chelsea Gem-pink', 'Favourite' (yellow and red), and 'Cloth of Gold' (yellow), but nowadays plants are usually offered merely under colour of flower descriptions.

CULTIVATION

The best way to start with lantanas is to buy a plant, which will usually have been raised from a cutting taken the previous year. If the plant consists mainly of new green growth it will have been a summer cutting, but if the growth is woody it will be a cutting from the previous spring.

If necessary shorten the shoots back to two pairs of leaves, assuming that your purchase has been made in spring, to give the plant a good shape and to make it bushy. Lantanas have a tendency to make straggly

Lantana camera hybrids have richly-coloured flowers which change colour as the flower develops.

growth, and any weak growths are better removed altogether. The pruning of the plant is most important if you wish to produce a well-balanced attractive flowering plant, and if it is done in late spring you will be rewarded with more prolific flowering in summer.

Lantanas are propagated by cuttings which are taken in the spring or autumn. They are taken in the usual way by cutting immediately below a node about 3–4 in (7.5–10 cm) from the growing tip. Remove all the leaves except the top pair and root in a suitable cutting compost using a hormone rooting powder to ensure success. Cover with a plastic dome or a polythene bag for about two weeks, and when it can

be seen that the cuttings have made some top growth they should be potted in 3½-in (9-cm) pots in compost E6 or JI No.2.

The new plants should be kept growing and need a minimum winter temperature of 50–55°F (10–13°C). If you cannot provide this requirement it is better to take spring cuttings only, and although these will not produce flowering plants during the season, due to the necessity of stopping the shoots, they will make excellent plants the following year. After potting the rooted cuttings they should be allowed to grow three or four pairs of leaves. The process is repeated until a nice bushy plant is formed.

Although lantanas are evergreen it is more convenient when growing them as greenhouse plants to allow them to become dormant in the winter. This is done by withholding water after the end of the summer and allowing the compost in the pot to dry out, but it should not be allowed to become dust-dry. Give it a very light watering from time to time during the winter months, particularly during any sunny spells.

This drying-out process causes the plant to shed all its leaves, and in this state it can be kept in the cool part of the greenhouse as it will tolerate temperatures as low as 35°F (2°C) without any harm.

By the end of the summer most of the stems of a spring cutting will have become woody, very similar to the growth of fuchsias, and mature plants grow quite a thick woody main stem which gives the plant a sturdy appearance.

By the end of the winter it is time to start the new season. The plants should be well watered, and as soon as tiny shoots of green growth are seen, just above the nodes, the branches should be cut back to two or three nodes, bearing in mind that the object is to build up a well-balanced shapely plant. Each plant should be treated according to its requirements by cutting out all weak growths and severely shortening branches which have made too much growth, and lightly pruning branches which have not made sufficient growth. As the new shoots develop it may be necessary to curb the growth of some, as lantanas do have a tendency to produce straggly growth.

Immediately after pruning, knock the plants out of their pots and remove all the old compost in the manner described for pelargoniums. Repot one-year-old plants in the same size of pot, which will usually be a 4½-in (11.5-cm) pot, and three-year-old plants in

6-in (15-cm) pots. Discard older plants altogether. In all cases use compost E6 or JI No.2, and, as soon as potted, water the plants but do not put them on watering trays until the roots are well established in the new compost, which will take about two or three weeks.

The flowers of lantanas appear singly or in pairs from the leaf axils close to the growing tips and are circular in shape, made up of delicately-formed florets in richly coloured shades of pink, red, orange and yellow, also pure white. They have a delightful characteristic of changing colour as the flowers develop. The leaves are tough and brittle to the touch and emit quite a strong scent. The plants like a good light and will, in fact, tolerate full sunshine on, say, a window-ledge in the house.

PELARGONIUMS
(Family Geraniaceae)

The order Geraniaceae is divided into five tribes, one of which is called Geraniae, which in turn also has five genera, two of which are *Geranium* and *Pelargonium*. It is at this point that the reader can become confused by virtue of the fact that gardeners still continue to refer to pelargoniums as geraniums despite botanists changing the name of the genus well over a hundred years ago. We therefore have two very different types of plants both being referred to by the same name, which can obviously create confusion.

The true geranium is a herbaceous hardy plant widespread throughout the world, in temperate regions and on mountains in the tropics, a considerable number being native to Great Britain, Europe and North America. On the other hand the pelargonium erroneously, but by common usage, called geranium, is a half-hardy plant found in temperate or subtropical regions of the world. About 90 per cent of the species grow in South Africa and others are found in Abyssinia, Kenya, Tanzania, Madagascar, Tristan du Cunha and New Zealand. During the last century pelargonium hybrids have become naturalised in some Mediterranean countries, the Canary Islands and in California. The species was first introduced to Europe in the seventeenth century by way of ships of the Dutch East India Company which established a naval station at Table Bay in South Africa in 1652. All the species grow in regions which have periods of drought, and often in areas where the soil is poor. Consequently, the species have developed the capacity to endure these conditions.

The genus *Pelargonium*, with which we are concerned, is divided into fourteen sub-genera, but only two of these are of interest in this context: *Ciconium* and *Pelargium*.

CICONIUM

It is from this sub-genus that the zonal pelargoniums, commonly called geraniums, are derived. As with many plants which have been raised from a number of different species by cross-breeding over a long period of time, it is impossible to be sure of the parents, which have been used to produce the many hybrids now in existence. Systematic breeding is a development of the twentieth century and few hybridists kept detailed records in earlier times; but it is traditionally thought that the main parent species used in developing the zonal hybrids were *Pelargonium inquinans* (introduced in 1714) and *Pelargonium zonale* (introduced in 1710), but it is more than likely that other species such as *P. scandens, P. frutetorum* and *P. hybridum* were also involved.

PELARGIUM

This sub-genus is the source of the regal pelargoniums. The main parent is thought to be the species *Pelargonium cucullatum*, with contributions from several other species including: *P. angulosum*, dark purple with darker streaks (introduced 1724); and *P. grandiflorum*, white with red streaks (introduced 1794).

In addition to zonal and regal pelargoniums there are several other groups, the main ones being ivy-leaved pelargoniums, scented-leaved, decorative foliage varieties, uniques and miniatures. You could easily fill a greenhouse with a small selection of the many varieties available, but if your purpose is to grow plants to furnish the house throughout the year it is necessary to show restraint and select the groups which will serve this purpose best. The two main groups, which are the zonals and regals, are therefore the obvious choice.

ZONAL PELARGONIUMS OR GERANIUMS (*P. hortorum*)

By 1860 hybridists were producing hybrids which could be said to be the forerunners of the modern geranium. A race of double flowers was produced in

Geranium 'Countess Mariza' is a free-flowering variety which is ideal as a pot plant.

1864 by the famous breeder Victor Lemoine, in his nursery at Nancy, which was the result of a sport. By 1869 Lemoine was listing 70 varieties of double-flowered geraniums. In 1871 a considerable cash prize was offered for the first double white, which gives some idea of the interest and the demand for geranium varieties. The most famous of all, 'Paul Crampel', was raised by Monsieur Crampel at his geranium nursery at Nancy. Realising he had raised a plant of considerable commercial value, he commenced propagating a large stock from cuttings, without allowing any of the plants to bloom, thus keeping secret the beauty of this new variety and reducing the possibility of theft. When he had filled several greenhouses and was ready to market the plant, it was allowed to bloom and introduced to the public in 1903. The plants were sold at over £1 each. At the time the red-flowered 'Henry Jacoby' was the most popular variety and Covent Garden was, as often, rather conservative, with the result that it was a few years before 'Paul Crampel' took pride of place, but eventually by 1910 it was recognised as the finest geranium in the world and has remained popular even to this day, despite the many superior cultivars which have since been raised.

Regal Pelargonium 'Aztec'.

REGAL PELARGONIUMS
(Pelargonium × domesticum)

The regal pelargonium, as we know it today with its ruffling of the petal, giving it the impression of being a double flower, was not developed until 1877. These pelargoniums are the most important of the genus, offering a much wider variety of colouring and form, and they make outstanding pot plants. For bedding-out purposes, however, they do not possess the virtues of the zonal pelargoniums.

Regal Pelargonium 'Hazel Cherry'.

Older varieties tend to have a much shorter flowering season than the zonals, which flower continuously throughout the summer months, but in recent years new varieties have been raised which flower almost continuously in the summer. In the USA regals are also known as 'Lady Washingtons' or 'Martha Washingtons' and in Germany as 'Edel-pelargoniums'.

Many of the regal and zonal pelargoniums grown at the turn of the century are still available today.

CULTIVATION

The growth requirements of both groups are very similar, consequently they can be treated as one group in this section. Pelargoniums are usually grown from cuttings; in fact until recent times they were always propagated from cuttings, except by hybridists raising new varieties from seed. However, during the last few years seedsmen have been offering new varieties of geraniums (zonal pelargoniums) in their seed catalogues which can easily be raised from seed, and will flower in the same season; consequently nowadays quite a large number of gardeners raise their plants from seed. On the other hand the best hybrids are named varieties, which can only be obtained from nurserymen, of which there are a number of firms who specialise in pelargoniums, and can offer a wide range of all groups, especially regals and zonals.

One of the virtues of pelargoniums is that they can be grown for a very low cost, in fact after the initial outlay the only expense involved is for compost, pots and enough heat to keep the greenhouse temperature from falling below $35-40°F$ ($2-5°C$) during any cold spells which may occur in the winter.

Cuttings can be taken in the spring or early autumn because at these times the growth is most active and the cutting will root quickly. Select strong shoots and cut these just below a node, which is the swelling on the stem at the leaf joint, giving a cutting about 3 in (7.5 cm) long. Remove all the leaves except the top two and also remove all the stipules (the leafy growths found at the base of the leaf stems), because these tend to rot, particularly those which may be in contact with the compost. The cutting is now prepared. Although the cuttings will root quite readily, pelargonium and geranium cuttings tend to develop a condition known as 'black-leg', which manifests itself by a blackening of the stem. If this occurs the cutting dies. Black-leg is caused by fungi,

Regal Pelargonium (*Pelargonium × domesticum*). Showing a few of the many named varieties available.

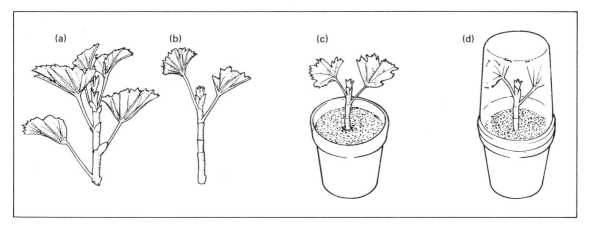

and it seems to occur more frequently when the cutting compost is kept too damp, or strangely enough conversely if the compost is allowed to become too dry. A cutting compost which I have found to give excellent results is a mixture of 3 parts of soilless cutting and sowing compost to 2 parts of vermiculite (see page 26).

Prepare the mixture the day before you are taking the cuttings, put it in the container you are going to use, then give it a good watering. Leave the cutting mixture exposed to the air in the propagator or for autumn cuttings, in the greenhouse, and by the following day the compost will be in the right condition to take the cuttings with the least risk of black-leg occurring. Vermiculite has the property of absorbing excess moisture and gradually releasing it to the soilless sowing and cutting compost as required, with the result that the cuttings never need watering while they are covered, and when the covering is removed the compost only needs watering very occasionally. It is necessary to cover the cuttings, otherwise on warm days they will wilt. If you use a standard size seed tray, with a plastic dome, this is ideal and will provide accommodation for about two

Fig. 6 Regal pelargonium cuttings. (a) An ideal cutting about 3 in (7.5 cm) long. (b) The prepared cutting after all the stipules and the surplus leaves have been removed. (c) The cutting inserted in the cutting compost to a depth of about 1 in (2.5 cm). (d) Cover with a plastic dome or a transparent plastic bag for seven to ten days.

dozen cuttings. If possible, keep the cuttings in a temperature of 60–65°F (15–18°C).

The cuttings should be in a good light but protected form the direct rays of the sun, and after ten to fourteen days remove the plastic cover. In five to six weeks all the cuttings should be well rooted and potted into 3½-in (9-cm) pots using compost E6. Pelargoniums require a slightly acid soil, pH 6.5 to 7. After potting, water the plants and do not water again until the surface of the soil indicates that watering is required. At this point it is necessary to differentiate between spring cuttings and autumn cuttings.

Fig. 7 A standard size plastic seed tray is ideal when a number of cuttings is required. (a) A tray full of regal pelargonium cuttings which have rooted. (b) Cuttings covered by a plastic dome. Moisture which forms during the night on the inside of the dome should be removed at the beginning of the day.

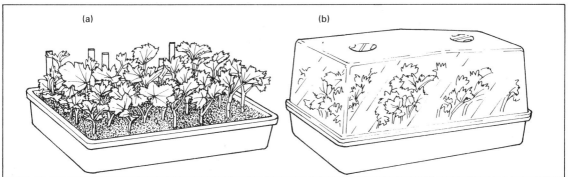

SPRING CUTTINGS

These can be taken from late winter to mid-spring depending on two factors: firstly whether you have the requisite shoots available, bearing in mind that mature plants are cut back severely in the autumn; and secondly when you require the plants to flower.

It is usual and desirable to prune severely both regals and zonals in autumn by cutting all shoots back to one or two nodes from the point of origin of the stem. This causes the dormant buds, which are located in the leaf axils, to break into growth, and during the winter months the plants slowly develop new shoots, with the result that by spring bushy plants have been formed. Usually by late winter these new shoots are too short to be suitable for cuttings and it is advisable to leave a few plants unpruned in the autumn of the varieties you wish to propagate in the spring. As soon as the cuttings have been taken, these plants are then cut back and will provide flowering plants to follow the autumn-pruned plants. This particularly applies to regals because zonal pelargoniums tend to flower more or less continuously.

The main object of taking spring cuttings of regals is to provide a batch of plants which will bloom after the autumn-raised plants have finished their first main show.

Fig.8 Regal pelargoniums should be heavily pruned in the autumn, each cut being above a node. The illustration shows a typical example of a plant after pruning.

Unlike zonal pelargoniums, which usually have only two or three flowers open at a time, regal pelargoniums develop buds on flowering stems, which all open within a week or two giving a mass of bloom over a period of some few weeks, after which there is a lull, with perhaps an odd bloom or two, then later in the summer they give another show of bloom. The second show is often as good as the first but varies according to the variety. Many of the older varieties only produce one good show, whereas some of the new varieties produce buds and flowers so continuously that it is difficult to find suitable growths for cuttings.

The best time to take cuttings is late winter or early spring. They should be kept in a propagator for about three to four weeks at 60–65°F (15–18°C), and then can go on the greenhouse bench, minimum temperature 45°F (7°C). Two weeks later they should be ready for potting into 3½-in (9-cm) pots in compost E6. As will be appreciated the rate of growth depends on the weather experienced and it is only possible to give approximate times. The plants themselves are the best guide; when roots begin to grow through the holes in the bottom of the pot, it is usually time to pot on into the next size, which is either a 4½-in (11.5-cm) or a 5-in (12.5-cm) pot. Be guided by the size of the plant. If it has made a lot of growth then pot into the larger size. For most varieties a 4½-in (11.5-cm) is quite large enough for a spring cutting plant. The main points in the cultivation of pelargoniums are the stopping and the feeding.

Soon after the cutting has been potted and made some growth it will have the appearance of a single stem with say five or six leaves. At this stage remove the growing point, which is at the tip of the stem or shoot. Use a pair of tweezers or sharp pointed nail scissors to ensure as little damage to the stem as possible.

The removal of the growing point will result in side shoots growing from the leaf axils, and when these are 2–2½ in (5–6.3 cm) long repeat the process which will create more side shoots, giving a nice bushy plant. This process is known as stopping. From now on allow the plant to grow without any further stopping, and in due course flower buds will develop. As soon as the tips of these flower buds show colour, it is necessary to commence feeding the plants. Use a high nitrogen feed in the quantity directed by the manufacturers and feed the plants once a week for two weeks and in the third week use a high potash feed. The reason for feeding the plants at this stage is to ensure that they have sufficient nitrogen and potassium available, otherwise the lower leaves will turn yellow and die by the time the plants are in full flower. In the case of regal pelargoniums you will find it necessary to tidy the plants from time to time by removing dead flowers and stalks etc. in order to keep the plants looking attractive, whereas with zonal pelargoniums it is usually only necessary to remove the dead flowers.

AUTUMN CUTTINGS

Cuttings of regals should be taken during late summer and zonals in early autumn. They will root more quickly than spring cuttings and should be potted in 3½-in (9-cm) pots in compost E6 as soon as ready. While in these pots the plants should be stopped, when ready, in the same way as for spring cuttings. The plants will usually be ready for stopping by late autumn.

By mid-winter they should be ready for potting on into 4½-in or 5-in (11.5 – 12-cm) pots. When the side shoots are 2 – 2½ in (5 – 6.3 cm) long, the second stop should be made, and with plants which have made sufficient growth a further stop should be made providing this can be done by the middle of spring.

Different varieties of regals vary quite considerably in growth. Some are short-jointed, i.e. the distance between the nodes is short, whereas others are long-jointed. Some are naturally bushy and when stopped will develop several side shoots, whereas others may only develop one or two side shoots. Each variety should be treated according to its individual requirements, bearing in mind that the object is to produce a well-shaped bushy plant with a good head of flowers. It never harms a plant to stop it, but it does, of course, delay the time of flowering, and if plants are required to flower in early summer the final stop should be not later than the middle of spring. Shoots should be allowed to grow at least 2 in (5 cm) before stopping, and if this length of growth has not been made it is better to allow the plant to grow unchecked.

Try to stop the plants at a node which has the dormant bud on the outside of the stem whenever possible, as this gives the plant a better shape.

By late summer regal pelargoniums have finished their useful flowering season, and when being grown on watering trays, which is by far the best method of growing all types of pelargoniums, these should be allowed to dry off. This will ensure that the compost in the pots is not damp when the plants are severely cut back to two or three nodes in autumn. When the plants have been pruned in this way, in some cases all the leaves will have been removed, leaving a plant consisting of short stems. In this state plants require very little water, particularly as they should be kept fairly dry throughout the winter. Do not allow the compost to become dust-dry, but on the other hand only water when the surface of the compost is dry to the touch, using a minimum of water.

If the plants are kept in this state they will withstand low temperatures without suffering any damage. A minimum temperature of 40°F (5°C) is quite satisfactory, and even without any greenhouse heating above 40°F day temperature on most days in the winter will be sufficient for slow steady growth.

In the following late winter the plants show many short green shoots, and are now ready for repotting. Knock the plants out of the pots by holding them upside down and bringing the rim of the pot into contact with a firm surface. The next step is to remove all the old compost with as little damage as possible to the roots, which you will find have become interlaced all round the outside and the bottom of the root-ball. A good method is to use a steel knitting needle, and by constantly prodding the mass of roots the compost is loosened to the extent that the root-ball can be squeezed between the hands, and after a little more prodding with the needle it will be found that shaking the plant will cause most of the compost to fall away from the roots, particularly if it is as dry as it should be.

It is impossible to avoid losing some of the roots, but if a good root system is still left on the plant no harm will be done.

Plants which have been in 4½-in (11.5-cm) pots should be repotted in 5-in (12.5-cm) pots, and plants in 5-in pots should be repotted into the same size of pot when they are eighteen-month-old plants (i.e. autumn cuttings from the year before the last summer). Older plants should be potted in 6-in (15-cm) pots. Plants which have been flowered for three seasons should be discarded. In all cases the plants are repotted in compost E6. It is not necessary to stop these repotted plants because the severe pruning the previous autumn will have stimulated a sufficient number of shoots to ensure bushy plants.

PRIMULA
(Family Primulaceae)

There are some 500 species in the genus *Primula* of which *P. obconica*, *P. sinensis* and *P. malacoides* are the most important for pot culture. Of lesser importance but useful as pot plants are primroses *(P. vulgaris)*, polyanthus *(P. vulgaris elatior)* and *P. kewensis*.

Primula malacoides was introduced into Great Britain in 1905 by George Forrest. The first introductions were a wishy-washy mauve pink, with small flowers and spindly growth, frail of habit, and with a deplorable tendency to rot at the crown of the plant at the slightest overwatering.

However, discerning nurserymen saw the possibilities inherent in the plant, and by a careful selection and breeding programme transformed the original species to a remarkable degree. By 1912 several hybrids possessing white and double flowers were recorded and two years later a very vigorous form with deep pink flowers was introduced. The hybrids available today are obtainable in pure white mauve, various shades of pink and deep red.

Primula obconica was introduced from China in 1880, where it was found in the Ichang gorge in 1879 by Charles Maries. The hybrids which have been raised from the original species are available in white, blue, salmon and crimson shades.

Primula sinensis, sometimes called the Chinese primula, was introduced from Canton, China, in 1820, but it was not until 1909 that large-flowered hybrids appeared.

Primula kewensis is not a true species but a hybrid which was produced by chance in the greenhouses of Kew Gardens in 1898.

As will be appreciated from the descriptions already given, much breeding of primulas took place during the first half of this century, and many of the hybrids raised were offered as named varieties. Nowadays, as with many other plants, the seedsmen offer packets of mixed colours, but some do still offer named varieties of *P. obconica* and *P. malacoides*.

Primula malacoides is known as the Fairy Primrose because of its dainty flowers.

CULTIVATION

Primulas are grown from seed sown in well-drained pots using JI seed compost or a soilless sowing compost. The seeds are very fine and should be sown on the surface, after which tap the pots lightly on a solid surface, so that the seeds settle into the compost. Do not shade the seed pans but leave exposed to the light, but not direct sunlight, covering with a sheet of glass or a plastic bag.

As soon as the seedlings are large enough to handle they should be pricked out into boxes, if you are growing a fair number, or alternatively into 3-in (7.5-cm) pots, using JI No.2 or equivalent. At this stage it is most important to ensure that the seedlings are planted at the correct height, i.e. the crown of the plant should be level with the surface of the soil.

If the crown is below the surface the plant will rot, and if above the surface it will not stand upright. The crown is the junction of the leaves with the stem. When the small pots are well-rooted, pot into 4-in (10-cm) or 4½-in (11-cm) pots, or if you have pricked out into boxes, transfer first of all to 3½-in (8.5-cm) and later to 4½-in (11-cm) pots. For this final potting use JI No.2 or compost E6.

The sowing and potting culture already described applies to all six of the primulas with which we are concerned, but the growth requirements differ slightly, and at this stage it is necessary to differentiate. *P. malacoides, P. kewensis* and *P. sinensis* are best sown from early to late spring; *P. obconica* from late winter to mid-spring; and polyanthus and primroses late spring to early summer.

Primula kewensis has fragrant yellow flowers.

All the primulas should be kept in a frame throughout the summer, and shaded from direct sunlight. At the beginning of autumn remove from the frame into the cool section of the greenhouse at first, until the weather becomes colder, then move *P. obconica, P. kewensis* and *P. malacoides* into the warmer section, where an average temperature of 45°F (7°C) is maintained. A drop to 40–42°F (4–5°C) on very cold nights will not damage the plants. On the other hand *P. sinensis* requires a higher temperature, about 50–55°F (10–13°C).

Polyanthus and primrose plants are kept in the cool section throughout the winter, as they are both hardy plants and will in fact stand frost.

Primulas are very useful plants for house decoration because not only are they attractive and colourful, but they flower from late winter to spring, a period during which flowering pot plants are not easy to find.

P. obconica will flower for months, but unfortunately has the disadvantage that it causes a skin rash to people who are allergic to the chemical secreted in the hairs on the underside of its leaves, and if you are one of these people always wear gloves when handling the plant.

All these primulas are treated as annuals and the greenhouse varieties are scrapped after flowering, but the polyanthus and primrose can be planted in the garden where they should bloom for years.

SAINTPAULIA
(Family Gesneriaceae)

Saintpaulia ionanthe is named after Walter von Saint Paul-Illaire, who found the species growing in East Africa, in 1893, when he was the District Governor of the former German Colony there. This is a plant which is nearly always referred to by its common name of African violet, and it is so well known that it is not really necessary to describe it.

African violets can be grown from seed but it is better to buy plants as, by this means, you can select plants in flower, choosing the flowers which have the greatest appeal to you. Plants grown from seed may not produce flowers which give you the same pleasure, and could prove disappointing, so if you only intend to grow a few plants, it is better to purchase plants in flower and propagate your further requirements by means of leaf cuttings.

Although these plants are called African violets, there are varieties with flowers in different shades of pink and red as well as violets and blues; there is also a white variety. In addition there are cultivars which have flowers with white-edged petals, and bicolours blue and white. There is also a considerable variation in the flowers themselves, including single flowers, double flowers, plain-edged petals, frilly-edged petals and so on.

Although many named varieties have been raised, nurserymen do not usually offer plants by name, so when selecting a plant you have to be guided by other considerations. The two main points to look for are thick flower stems, as this usually means that the plant will be floriferous, and dark green leaves. One of the many causes of losses when growing African violets is the plant rotting, and plants with light green leaves are more likely to suffer from this complaint.

Saintpaulia ionantha is better known as the African Violet, despite many of the hybrids having pink, red, blue or white flowers.

CULTIVATION

As the plants are slow-growing they can usually be grown in the same pot for two years. They have rather small fibrous roots and do well in a soilless potting compost. Plants which have been purchased or potted on will not require feeding for the first year, but in the second year you might find it necessary to feed with a balanced liquid fertilizer, every three or four weeks, if the plant does not appear to be making any new growth.

African violets are not easy plants to grow in the house and it is necessary to strive to provide the conditions they require in regard to light, heat and atmosphere. The first requirement for continuous flowering is good light. Like most flowering pot plants the African violet must be kept out of direct sunlight in the spring, summer and early autumn, at times when the sun is hot, otherwise the leaves will burn.

In the house, windows facing west, north or east should prove suitable in the summer months, but in the winter a south-facing window would probably prove more suitable.

The ideal growing temperature is around 70°F (21°C) during the day, and 55–60°F (13–15°C) during the hours of darkness, but when growing at these temperatures it is essential to avoid the atmosphere becoming too dry.

One of the main difficulties in meeting with success with this plant, in the house, is that it requires a really humid atmosphere to thrive. When the air temperature inside a room in a house is 70°F (21°C), the air is far too dry for the plant's requirements and it is necessary to try to provide some local moisture in the air in the immediate vicinity of the plant.

A good way of doing this is to put a layer of pebbles, about 1 in (2.5 cm) deep, in a bowl and pour water in the bowl to just below the level of the pebbles. Stand the plant pot on the pebbles, in the centre of the bowl, and the water constantly evaporating all round the plant should provide sufficient moisture to keep it happy.

Perhaps the best procedure to adopt with African violets is to experiment by putting plants in different positions in the house, to ascertain where the plant thrives best. One of the main reasons for the loss of African violets is the rotting of the plants, and this is often caused by overwatering. The amount of water a plant needs, and the frequency of watering, depends on the temperature in which the plant is growing, and also the humidity of the air. Obviously the plant will need to be watered more frequently when growing in a warm dry living room, but even in these conditions it is better to allow the surface of the compost to become dry before watering the plant. Far more plants are lost by overwatering than by underwatering. The African violet is sensitive to the temperature of the water and tepid water should be used; moreover, there should not be any appreciable difference in the temperature of the water between one watering and another. Do not water with cold water on one occasion and tepid water on another occasion. If you keep a full watering-can in a warm room, and always use this after it has been standing for about 24 hours, and only water when the plant requires it, you are not likely to lose any plants.

Should you find that your plants cease to flower, this can be due to several causes. The most likely cause is insufficient light, but it can also be due to the plant not liking its surroundings, the air being too dry or the temperature being too low, or both. Often plants cease flowering in the winter because the daylight is too poor; you can overcome this by giving the plants artificial illumination. African violets are very responsive to artificial light and can be grown very effectively solely by this means. A good source of light to use is warm-white fluorescent tubular lights, which should be placed about 12 in (30 cm) above the plants for 12 to 14 hours per day.

Propagation of African violets is by leaf cuttings, which should be taken in winter, if you are prepared to provide a temperature of 65–70°F (18–21°C), otherwise delay until spring, when the day temperatures will be warmer. Select a leaf from the second or third row, from the outside, and remove it, complete with its stem. Insert the stem about ¼ in (6 mm) deep in the cutting compost and enclose the pot in a plastic bag, until you can see growth appearing from the base of the leaf stalk.

A mixture of equal parts of peat and sharp sand makes a good cutting compost. Depending on the growing conditions, it will take some four to seven weeks before a clump of plantlets can be seen, and when the individual plantlets are large enough they should be separated from each other and potted in soilless potting compost, in 2½-in (6-cm) pots.

The first growth of the cutting is a rosette of leaves

which lies flat on the surface, but subsequent rows grow more erect.

It is better to cut off the first flower stems which appear, if you have sufficient patience, because you will be rewarded by a better display from the next batch of flowers. It usually takes about a year for a cutting to produce a good flowering plant.

SCHLUMBERGERA, RHIPSALIDOPSIS AND EPIPHYLLUM
(Family Cactaceae)

These plants are members of the cactus family and are often referred to as succulents. Owing to classification changes made by taxonomists, over the years, it is very easy to become confused when referring to *Schlumbergera* and *Rhipsalidopsis* by their botanical names; consequently, this is one of the few instances when it is preferable to identify the plants by their common names, which are Christmas Cactus and Easter Cactus. The other division referred to in the heading is usually just called an epiphyllum.

CHRISTMAS CACTUS
Originally this species was known as *Epiphyllum truncatum*, and in the nineteenth-century gardening books it was always referred to by this name. Later the name was changed to *Zygocactus truncatus*, commonly known as the Christmas cactus, because it will flower naturally at Christmas (in the northern hemispere), given the right conditions. According to modern classification the species is now called *Schlumbergera truncata*, but as with many species which are widely known under a name which has been well established, it is easy enough to change the name but very difficult to get the majority of gardeners to use the new nomenclature, and consequently most gardeners still refer to the Christmas cactus by its old name of *Zygocactus truncatus*.

The species is a native of Brazil, but nowadays all the plants offered for sale are hybrids. Much hybridising took place in the nineteenth century and plants were usually sold as named varieties in quite a wide range of colours, such as deep rose, reddish-orange, purple, and whites with coloured edges (e.g. white edged with rose, white with purple margin). Today, plants are not usually offered in named varieties and mostly only red shades are available.

The Christmas and Easter cacti do not have true leaves. The leaf-like portions are really flattened stems and, as the plants grow larger, they gradually become cylindrical.

As plants grown from seed take some four to eight years to reach flowering size it is usual to buy plants already in flower which will, of course, be during the winter. During the winter months plants will require a minimum temperature of 35°F (2°C) to survive, but to maintain growth require 55–65°F (13–18°C).

The flowering period is during early and mid-winter, after which the plants should be kept watered until late summer. During this period feed the plant with a weak liquid fertiliser, and in the summer months it is best to keep the plants outside but protected from the direct rays of the sun.

The plant makes growth at the tip of each segment or pad, and as the stems grow longer they tend to droop; therefore it should be staked at an early age to encourage a more upright growth.

Watering of the plants should be discontinued at the beginning of autumn and the plants kept on the dry side until flowering buds appear, when watering should be recommenced. The purpose of withholding water is to allow the plants to rest; and it also seems to stimulate the initiation of flower buds. Bring the plants indoors at the end of the summer but keep them in a cool place until the buds are well-formed, when they should then be given warmer conditions – minimum 60°F (15°C).

The best time to repot is shortly after the plant has flowered, using a soilless compost suitable for ericaceous plants, because schlumbergeras like an acid compost. Repotting is usually only necessary every other year and the plant should be left undisturbed unless it is pot-bound. Always use the smallest size of pot possible.

This is also the best time to take cuttings. Sever the top three segments at the end of a branch, and insert ½ in (13 mm) deep in moist peat, covering the pot with a plastic dome or bag until the cutting has rooted, which should be in about three to four weeks. Allow the cuttings to dry for two or three days before

inserting in the rooting medium, otherwise they tend to rot.

Rhipsalidopsis gaertneri, the Easter Cactus, with its bright red flowers, will bloom freely in the house.

EASTER CACTUS

This species was originally known as *Schlumbergera gaertneri*, but its new name is *Rhipsalidopsis gaertneri*. The plants offered for sale are, of course, hybrids which have been developed from the species. The flowers which appear on the tips of the stems are various shades of red ranging from pink to crimson. The plants, in form, are similar to the Christmas cactus, having leaf-like stems which tend to droop unless supported.

The cultivation of the Easter cactus is the same as for the Christmas cactus, except that the watering and resting periods are at different times. The Easter cactus blooms naturally during late spring, so the rest period, when watering is reduced to a minimum, is during late winter and early spring; otherwise give the plant the same treatment as you would a Christmas cactus.

EPIPHYLLUMS

These are much larger plants than the foregoing and the flowers they produce are much larger and more showy. The plants offered for sale are hybrids between the various species, in particular *Epiphyllum ackermannii*, which comes from Mexico, Central America and South America.

The natural flowering time of the epiphyllum is early summer; consequently you will probably purchase a plant at this time. After flowering the plant is best kept in a shady spot, in a good light.

At the end of the summer bring the plant indoors or into the greenhouse. Water normally from the flowering period until the end of autumn, and then withhold water to give the plants a resting period, until the first signs of the flower buds, which should be some time in early spring. Do not allow the compost to dry out completely, but water very sparingly and keep it well on the dry side. During this resting period the plants should be kept in a cool atmosphere, at about 45–50°F (7–10°C). As soon as

pot is full of roots. Use the smallest size of pot compatible with the root system and only transfer to a larger pot when necessary.

The propagation of epiphyllums is by cuttings, because like the Christmas cactus it takes four to eight years for plants to flower when grown from seed. Select a healthy terminal growth of the leaf-like stems and remove the top 5–6 in (13–15 cm), making a

Epiphyllum.

the flower buds are visible put the plants in a warmer temperature, minimum 60°F (15°C), and commence watering again. Feed every two weeks with a high potash fertiliser until the first flowers open.

Repotting, if necessary, should be carried out shortly after the plants have finished flowering, using soilless compost of the type suitable for ericaceous plants, because epiphyllums require an acid compost free from lime. Do not repot plants before they are pot-bound, as an epiphyllum flowers best when its

clean cut with a knife. Allow the cutting to dry off for two or three days and then push the cut end into moist peat, ½ in (13 mm) deep, and support it with a thin stake. Cover the pot with a plastic dome or enclose in a plastic bag for two or three weeks and keep in a minimum temperature of 60°F (15°C) until it is well rooted when it should be potted in the compost in a 2½-in (6-cm) or 3-in (9-cm) pot.

The growth of epiphyllums is much more erect than the Christmas cactus and plants should be kept staked from the time of taking the cutting, to encourage the plant to remain erect; otherwise it tends to sprawl, owing to the weight of the young stems. Plants can be grown on for years. The flowers of epiphyllums are usually shades of red, but there are also hybrids with flowers in white, pink, cream and purple or mauve.

If you grow epiphyllums in the house, on a windowledge, it is advisable to avoid moving them once the flower buds have formed, because the buds

An *Epiphyllum* makes an attractive decoration in a hanging basket.

are drawn towards the light. If a plant is turned the buds will obviously have to change direction and this weakens them to the extent that you get quite a number of buds dropping off the plant. This does not apply in the greenhouse because there is sufficient light all round the plant. Once all the buds have opened into flowers the plant can be moved without detriment. The same remarks apply to the Christmas cactus and the Easter cactus.

SMITHIANTHA
(Family Gesneriaceae)

Smithianthas are very attractive plants with ornamental leaves, which have a velvety texture mainly green in colour with brown markings along the veins, above which the flower spikes rise to a height of some 12 – 18 in (30 – 45 cm)

The tubular bell-shaped flowers, which hang down on short stalks all round the main stems, are bright shades of pink, orange, red and yellow. The inside of the flower is a different colour from the outside and is delicately patterned or mottled, so that you may have, say, a red flower with a speckled orange interior, and the overall effect is most attractive. It is the flowers which give the plant the common name of temple bells. The genus was named after a Matilda Smith, who was a botanical artist attached to Kew Gardens. Smithianthas are closely related to gesnerias and their correct nomenclature has been somewhat confused. They used to be known as naegelias and some nurserymen still offer then under this name. Their native habitat is Mexico. Only the hybrids are grown nowadays, and these are usually offered as mixed colours, but at one time there were named varieties available.

Their natural flowering time is autumn, and, as there are few flowering pot plants sufficiently obliging to produce their flowers during these months, it is a pity that smithianthas are not more well-known and more widely-grown.

Smithianthas are tuberous-rooted plants, and the tubers or rhizomes form at the base of the main stem. The tubers are an elongated cone shape, with a white scaly appearance and usually about ½ – 1 in (13 – 25 mm) long. Each plant produces an average of some three tubers by the end of the season, and, as each tuber will produce a new plant the following year, you can appreciate that there is no need to propagate by any other means in order to maintain a collection of these plants. Smithianthas can be grown from seed or tubers, but as the latter are usually obtainable it is preferable to buy tubers.

CULTIVATION
The time to start the tubers into growth is late winter or early spring, but the point to bear in mind is that a

temperature of 65°F (18°C) is initially required, and when the shoots appear a minimum temperature of 55°F (13°C) is needed for growth to continue. Tubers started in late winter will usually bloom in late summer and early autumn. Tubers started in spring will bloom in autumn. If you do not have the facilities to maintain a minimum temperature of 55°F (13°C) during early spring it is better to delay potting until mid-spring so that the shoots do not appear until the weather is warmer.

Make sure the compost is moist but not wet and do not water until absolutely necessary, as too much moisture at this stage before any appreciable root

growth has occurred can result in tuber rotting. Place the pots in a temperature of 65°F (18°C) until shoots appear, after which the plants can be moved to a slightly cooler place. A temperature of 60°F (15°C) is ideal.

The tuber should be placed on its side in the compost about ½ in (13 mm) below the surface, using JI potting compost No.2 or compost E6. Pot four tubers in a 5 or 6-in (12.5 or 15-cm) half-pot, which is quite adequate for the root run, and gives a better balance of pot to flower.

Apart from watering as required, the plants do not require any further attention until they have flowered. When grown in a greenhouse they should be given light shading in the late spring and summer

Smithianthas are sometimes called Temple Bells. They have attractive flowers and beautiful velvety leaves.

months. When the plants have finished flowering, they should be allowed to dry off gradually until the leaves begin to wither away, at which stage withhold water altogether, and allow the compost in the pots to become completely dry. The pots can be stored under the bench in the greenhouse (providing you can maintain a minimum temperature of 45°F/7°C on average), laying each pot on its side.

The tubers will not come to any harm with an occasional short spell at 40°F (4°C) if the pots are bone dry, but should not be kept in temperatures below 45°F (7°C) for weeks on end.

At the end of the winter knock the soil out of the pots and carefully sort out the tubers, which should then be started into growth as already described.

SOLANUM
(Family Solanaceae)

Solanum capsicastrum, when grown as a pot plant, is a dwarf evergreen shrub about 12–18 in (30–45 cm) in height, which produces most attractive fruit resembling small bright red cherries. It is commonly known as winter cherry, or Christmas cherry. This popular plant for winter decoration is readily obtainable, and as it can be grown on for at least a second year, or alternatively propagated from

Solanum capsicastrum, the Christmas or Winter Cherry, owes its attraction to its bright red berries.

89

cuttings, it is not really necessary to grow it from seed.

CULTIVATION

To grow plants from seed sow in mid-winter at 68−78°F (20−25°C) and provide an adequate temperature of 60−70°F (15−21°C) while the young seedlings are developing.

Propagation by cuttings is carried out in spring, taking stem cuttings about 2−3 in (5−7.5 cm) long and, after stripping off all but the top three or four leaves, insert the stem of the cutting about ½ in (13 mm) deep in the cutting compost. It is always beneficial to dip the cuttings in a hormone rooting compound as this speeds up the formation of the roots.

When the young plants are growing in the spring they should be kept bushy by pinching out the growing tips from time to time. Whether growing seedlings or cuttings the first potting will be into 3 or 3½-in (7.5 or 9-cm) pots followed by a final potting in 4 or 5½-in (10 or 14-cm) pots, in both instances using compost E6 or JI potting compost No.2.

By early summer the plants should be in flower and at this stage it is better to keep them outside, in a position where they are shaded from the midday sun, in the hope that the flowers will be pollinated by the insects, rather than in the greenhouse, where insects are not encouraged. The crop of berries the plant will produce is entirely dependent on how well the flowers are pollinated. While the plants are flowering it is essential that the pots are kept well watered, and not allowed to dry out. The star-shaped flowers are white, and although numerous they are so small that they appear insignificant.

When the berries have developed satisfactorily the plants can then be brought inside the greenhouse which will speed up the growth. The berries when first formed are green in colour and they gradually change through yellow and orange to the ultimate familiar orange-red colour.

Solanums require plenty of light but they last longer if kept in a temperature range of 50−60°F (10−16°C) during the autumn and winter months.

The best time to buy a plant is in the autumn when it is bearing yellow to red berries and you are able to see how well-laden it is. The following spring, after taking any cuttings you require, the plants should be pruned by cutting back the stems to about half their length; and, as soon as new growth appears, either pot on into a larger size pot or preferably remove the old compost from the roots and repot in new compost.

STREPTOCARPUS
(Family Gesneriaceae)

This attractive plant, commonly known as the Cape primrose, is a native of South Africa. There are several species in cultivation of which there are two types: stemless and stemmed. It is the hybrids which

have been developed from the stemless species that are grown as pot plants for the house and greenhouse. Of the stemless hybrids there are two main types, namely plants which form only one large leaf, and plants which form several leaves of similar size arranged in the form of a rosette.

The flowers, which are funnel-shaped, flaring out to a five-lobed open mouth, are fairly large and are borne on wiry stems about 10 in (25 cm) high, usually two or three flowers on each stem. The flowers have a wide range of colour in shades of red, blue, lilac purple, pink and white often with a throat veined in a contrasting colour. The modern streptocarpus is a vast improvement on the species and the old varieties,

and is a beautiful and most useful flowering pot plant as it has such a long flowering period.

CULTIVATION

The best way of starting a collection of streptocarpus plants is to raise them from seed, which is easily obtainable. Plants can be raised from seed without difficulty, whether you possess a greenhouse or not, because seed can be sown at any time between mid-winter and mid-summer. Seed sown in mid-winter in a temperature of 68–78°F (20–25°C) should

Streptocarpus. A group of modern hybrids which have larger flowers and are much more free-flowering than the old types.

produce flowering plants in summer. Alternatively, seed may be sown in early summer without heat to produce flowering plants for the following year. If you can it is better to sow seeds in mid-winter, because not only will these produce plants which will flower the first year but by the following year they will be much larger plants and will usually provide a continuous mass of flowers from mid-summer until early winter. The seed should be sown on the surface

of a soilless seed compost and, either pressed into the compost, or covered very lightly with a fine sand. If you decide to press the seed into the compost, use an implement to which the seeds will not adhere and, after completing the operation, wet the surface slightly with water, by means of a fine spray, which will help to bed the seeds down in the compost. Enclose the seed pan in a plastic bag until the first signs of germination, which should be in 12 – 14 days if the temperature has been between 68 and 78°F (20 – 25°C).

Streptocarpus.

The seedlings should then be pricked out into 4½-in (11.5-cm) half-pots as soon as they are large enough to handle – the sooner the better – using compost E6. The seedlings are very slow-growing but when they are about three months old should be large enough to pot into 2½-in (6-cm) pots in compost E6. Potting on is only necessary when the pots are full of roots, and this will vary from plant to plant, but the size of the top growth is usually a good indication. When the plant has made good leaf growth it is time to look at the root growth. Your plants are not likely

consequently the plants remain in a dormant condition and tend to lose their larger leaves.

Once you have raised a batch of plants from seed you can propagate the best plants by means of leaf cuttings. Propagation of plants by leaf cuttings is carried out either by cutting the leaf across into three or four sections and pushing the cut edge of the leaf into the cutting compost about ½ in (13 mm) deep, or by dividing along the central vein and inserting the cut edge of the leaf obliquely to a depth of ½ in (13 mm). Plantlets should grow from the bottoms of

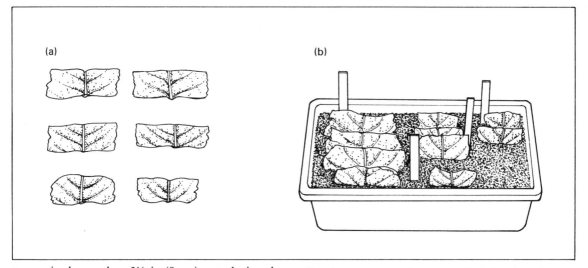

to require larger than 3½-in (9-cm) pots during the first year, from seed sown in mid-winter to early spring, but the following spring should be ready for potting on into 4½-in (11.5-cm) or 5-in (13-cm) pots. Be guided by the size of the plant and the amount of root growth both for when to pot and for the size of pot to use.

Ideally the plants should be grown in a light airy atmosphere averaging about 65°F (18°C) and lightly shaded from strong sunlight. Given these conditions plants will continue growing the whole year round and will also flower for about three-quarters of the time. The usual procedure, however, is to allow the plants to dry off, after the middle of autumn, and from then onwards they are kept as dry as possible, without being allowed to dry out completely until growth is re-started in the spring. In this dry state plants can be wintered in the greenhouse at temperatures as low as 40 – 45°F (5 – 7°C) without harm. Streptocarpus make little or no growth at temperatures below 60°F (15°C) especially when dry;

Fig.9 Streptocarpus can be propagated by leaf cuttings. (a) 1 – 2 in (2.5 – 5 cm) sections cut from a healthy leaf are pressed into the cutting compost (b) to a depth of ½ in (1 cm) and kept totally enclosed under a plastic dome or bag for a few weeks, until roots have grown. In due course tiny plants will form at the base of the leaf.

the sections in about 4 to 6 weeks, and when they have made sufficient root they should be detached and potted in 2½-in (6-cm) pots.

If you wish to keep a continuous stock of streptocarpus it is as well to raise a few new plants each year, either from seed or from cuttings, because although they are perennials plants grown in pots do not usually thrive after the third or fourth year, and even if they do they become too big and require too big a pot to be useful for house decoration. A well-grown plant will require a 6-in (15-cm) pot in its third or fourth year, after which it will require an even larger pot; therefore plants should be discarded after the fourth year, as a general rule, unless you have some special reason for keeping a plant.

Browallia speciosa 'Blue Troll' flowers profusely over several weeks.

PLANTS TO GROW FROM SEED

BROWALLIA (FAMILY SOLANACEAE)

Of the nine species which have been found, it is *Browallia speciosa* from which the modern hybrids have been developed. Although it has the common name of bush violet, varieties are available with blue, lavender and white flowers.

In appearance it is a shrubby plant about 12–20 in (30–50 cm) in height, freely branching, flowering profusely over several weeks, not unlike *Exacum affine* in habit. The flowers, which are about 2 in (5 cm) across, are tubular, flaring out to five petals and usually have a white throat; the 1 in (2.5 cm) long stalks, carrying the flowers, are produced from the leaf axils. It is a very useful pot plant because it can be brought into flower during the late summer and autumn; or, if the sowing is delayed, it will flower during the winter and early spring.

Seed should be sown in JI seed compost or soilless seed compost, lightly covered with compost, and the seed pan enclosed in a polythene bag or covered with a sheet of glass. Ideal temperature for germination is 60–65°F (15–18°C) which should result in the seedlings making their appearance in 14 to 21 days. The time of flowering is governed by the time the seeds are sown. Sow in late winter or early spring for plants to flower in late summer and autumn. If you wish to grow plants for winter flowering sow in late spring.

When the seedlings are large enough to handle, pot in 3-in (7.5-cm) pots using compost E6 or equivalent, and in due course pot on into 4 or 4½-in (10 or 11-cm) pots, depending on the size of the plants.

Browallias have a tendency to become leggy and to prevent this it is necessary to pinch out the growing points regularly to produce bushy compact plants. The plants produce a succession of flowers; you will need to remove dead flowers from time to time to keep the plants looking attractive. If the plants are allowed to grow naturally they make good subjects for hanging baskets because they develop an arching habit.

The ideal temperature range for browallias is 50–60°F (10–15°C) during the flowering season. Temperatures higher than 65°F (18°C) will shorten the life of the flowers and the flowering period. In the house the plant should be kept in a cool room, in the window, where it is exposed to bright light, and it will benefit from some direct sunlight in the late autumn and winter months. Browallias are annuals and should be discarded when they have finished flowering.

CAMPANULA (FAMILY CAMPANULACEAE)

Until quite recently *Campanula isophylla*, commonly known as Star of Bethlehem, was always propagated by cuttings, when grown by amateur gardeners, but a new variety called 'Kristal' is now available which can be grown from seed. *Campanula isophylla* has a trailing habit, and unless it is being grown in a hanging basket it needs support.

Sow seed in early spring, heat 60–65°F (15–18°C), in soilless compost and keep covered by glass or in a polythene bag until seedlings begin to appear, then expose to full light but not sunshine. Prick out into 2-in (5-cm) pots as soon as the seedlings are large enough to handle. When the plants are ready to be potted on, use a 4½-in (11-cm) pot, potting two or three plants to each pot, in compost E6 or equivalent. As the plants grow, give them any support which may be necessary to give the effect you desire. There are many different types of support available.

Campanula isophylla is a cool-house plant and enjoys outside conditions in the summer more than the conditions in a greenhouse or a house; therefore it should be put in the coolest place available in the house which is compatible with its light requirements (bright light shaded from direct sunlight). Do not allow the compost to dry out, but on the other hand do not overwater. Ideal temperatures are 60–65°F (15–18°C) during the summer, and 40–45°F

Campanula isophylla is an ideal plant for a hanging basket.

(5–7°C) during the winter when the plants are resting, keeping the compost on the dry side, not too moist and not too dry.

Plants can be grown on year after year and new plants can easily be raised from cuttings, which should be taken when the plants have made some new growth in the spring. Take tip cuttings, 2 in (5 cm) long, with three or four pairs of leaves, the stem being cut below a node. Remove the lowest pair of leaves, dip the stem in a hormone rooting powder and insert about ½ in (13 mm) deep into the cutting compost. Keep the cuttings enclosed until some new growth is observed, when they can be left uncovered until they are ready to be potted.

CINERARIA (FAMILY COMPOSITAE)

Although most gardeners refer to these plants as cinerarias their correct name is *Senecio*. The species *Senecio cruentus* comes from the Canary Islands where it grows as a perennial. It was introduced into England about 200 years ago and is the main parent from which today's cineraria hybrids have been raised.

Owing to the fact that cinerarias bloom in the winter and spring months, they have always been very popular plants. An enormous number of hybrids

96

have been raised, which offer such variety in both size of plant and shape of flower that plants are available to meet any grower's requirements.

Cinerarias tend to have very large leaves, and if the larger varieties are grown the plants take up far too much room in the frame and greenhouse. For house decoration it is better to grow the dwarf or compact plants.

In appearance a cineraria in flower looks rather like a bouquet of daisy-type flowers surrounded by bright green leaves. The colour range of the flowers is enormous and includes many different shades of reds, pinks, maroons, blues, orange and white in self-colours and bi-colours. There is also a variety with star-like flowers.

Cinerarias have been very popular plants since early Victorian times and during the latter part of the nineteenth century, when many professional gardeners were engaged in raising new and improved cultivars or hybrids, there were many named varieties offered by nurserymen. It is not surprising that they have always been popular plants because not only are they attractive and colourful flowering plants, but

with careful planning they can be flowered from autumn to spring; also, in a cool atmosphere of say 45 – 55°F (7 – 13°C), some varieties will remain in flower for six to eight weeks.

Although they are perennials, cinerarias are usually treated as annuals and are grown from seed each year, the plants being discarded after flowering.

Most seed growers or merchants offer their own strains, which are usually mixed colours, and these vary from dwarf plants, about 10 in (25 cm) in height, to large plants, 18 in (45 cm) tall. It is, however, not so much the height as the width which makes the plant large, because the taller varieties have large leaves and well-grown plants measure about 2 ft (60 cm) in diameter, taking up a considerable amount of room on the greenhouse bench. Unless you have a lot. of room to spare it is better to grow the large-flowered dwarf varieties, which are in any case more useful for house decoration.

Sow the seed in either a soilless compost or in JI

A *Cineraria* is a very colourful plant for winter and early spring flowering.

seed compost covering lightly with a fine layer of the compost or fine sand. Cover the seed pan with a sheet of glass or enclose it in a plastic bag. Seed sown in mid-spring should be kept in a temperature of about 60–65°F (15–18°C) and germination should take about seven days, in which case a fortnight after sowing the seedlings should be ready for pricking out into trays using compost E6.

In a further three to four weeks the seedlings should be ready for potting into 3-in (7.5-cm) pots and when these are well rooted in mid-summer pot on into 4½ or 5-in (11.5 or 13-cm) pots, depending on the size of the plant.

Seed sown in spring, as described, should produce

Cineraria is easily raised from seed in a very wide range of colours.

plants which have been potted into their final pots by mid-summer and these will bloom from the beginning of autumn onwards. Plants from the same sowing do not all bloom at the same time, and if you grow, say, a dozen plants from a spring sowing, they will probably cover a period of about three months, i.e. from the end of the summer until early winter. Seed can be sown any time between mid-spring and early summer inclusive; consequently, by sowing at different times,

plants can be had in flower throughout the autumn and winter months.

Cinerarias can be grown in soilless compost, but in my experience they grow better in compost E6. Having large leaves, they require frequent watering in hot sunny weather and should always be shaded from direct sunlight. Even so, the leaves will nearly always flag during the heat of the day despite the compost being well watered, but in the cool of the evening they will recover and will be none the worse. It is, however, better to grow the plants outside in the summer, as soon as all danger of frost has passed. Any situation where the light is good, but out of the direct rays of the sun, is suitable. Before the end of the summer the plants should be taken indoors or preferably into a greenhouse.

As the plants make considerable growth in their growing period, feeding should commence after the plants have been in their final pots for some four or five weeks.

Cinerarias tend to attract greenfly and whitefly in the summer months so, from time to time, inspect the undersides of the leaves and spray with a suitable insecticide if it is necessary.

After the plants have finished flowering they should be discarded as they do not make satisfactory flowering plants in the second year.

GERBERA (FAMILY COMPOSITAE)

This plant originates from South Africa as its common name of Transvaal daisy implies. It is a half-hardy perennial which flowers from mid-summer to autumn. The daisy-like flowers are very attractive in a wide range of colours (including pink, rose, red, salmon orange and pale yellow) on strong stems, and are excellent as cut flowers.

Up to recent times the Jamesonii hybrids, which have flower stems about 1½–2 ft (45–60 cm) high, were used for pots, but a new variety has been introduced called 'Happipot New'. This has stems about 8–12 in (20–30 cm), long with flowers about 3½ in (9 cm) across, and makes a much more compact and attractive pot plant. This new variety will flower about four months after sowing.

Sow gerbera seeds in mid-spring in JI seed compost or soilless compost, by just pressing the seed into the surface of the compost. Put the seed pan in the propagator, temperature 65–70°F (18–21°C), and cover with a sheet of glass, leaving exposed to full light. A fortnight after sowing the seedlings should be ready for pricking out into a seed tray, using compost E6 or equivalent. Three weeks later they should be ready for potting in 3½-in (9-cm) pots and later, when sufficiently grown, into 5 or 6-in (13 or 15-cm) pots, depending on the size of the individual plant, again using compost E6.

Gerberas are very easy to grow and do not require any special treatment. Plants can be kept in the greenhouse on watering trays or outside in the open air during the summer, in which event they should be watered as required. The compost in the pots should not be allowed to become too wet and should be watered regularly but sparingly.

Having raised a batch of gerberas from seed you will no doubt have raised enough plants to meet your requirements, and the following season it will only be necessary to repot the previous year's crop. Gerberas are perennials and each year will grow larger; by the third year they will require a 10-in (25-cm) pot, but as they are so easy to raise from seed it is really better to raise a new batch every two or three years.

Pots as large as 10-in (25-cm) are too cumbersome for house pot plants; they also take up too much room in the greenhouse, and gerberas have to be protected from the frost. During the winter, cease watering the pots but do not allow the compost to get too dry. Just water sparingly when the surface of the compost looks dry and the pots are beginning to feel a bit on the light side.

Gerbera jamesonii, the Transvaal Daisy, has a very attractive flower in various shades of pink, red, orange and yellow.

Freesia hybrids are both colourful and fragrant.

BULBS

Space is always at a premium in all active greenhouses and any plants which have a resting period are most welcome, particularly if they flower at a time when flowering pot plants are somewhat scarce. The subjects dealt with in this section have the added advantage that they are permanent members of the greenhouse stock, in fact having made the initial purchase no further outlay is necessary.

The original bulbs will flower each year for a number of years, and from time to time offsets are formed which can easily be grown on to produce flowering-size bulbs.

FREESIA (FAMILY IRIDACEAE)

Freesias are half-hardy plants which grow from corms and flower in the spring. They can be grown from seed, but it is more satisfactory to start with corms, which are quite inexpensive and will flower in six months from planting.

They are not grown as pot plants but for use as cut flowers, and a convenient way to grow them is to plant six corms in a 6-in (15-cm) pot planting each corm 1 in (2.5 cm) deep and about 2 in (5 cm) apart using compost E6 or the equivalent. Freesia leaves are sword-like, similar to gladiola leaves, and, as they grow about 3½ ft (1 m) in height, require some support.

The method I use is to push three 3-ft (90-cm) canes into the compost, at the side of the pot, equidistant from each other, and when the leaves are about 6 in (15 cm) tall, tie a piece of garden twine round the three canes, which has the effect of holding the leaves within the confines of the canes.

As the plants grow, more ties are made, right up to the top of the canes. After planting the corms, water the compost and then only sparingly until growth has been made and the leaves are well through the surface.

Freesias must be grown in a cool atmosphere if strong healthy growth is to be achieved. A planting in late summer, grown in a cold greenhouse which is only frost-proof, will usually provide flowers from the middle of spring.

Ideally freesias should be grown in a greenhouse with a minimum temperature of 40°F (4°C). They can be forced into earlier bloom, but care must be taken to avoid soft growth developing by using too high a temperature.

When the plants have finished flowering, keep watering the pots until the foliage shows signs of dying down, or until early summer, then cease watering altogether and place the pots in the full sun in the greenhouse with the object of ripening the corms. Remove the dead foliage when necessary.

Freesias can be started into growth any time from mid-summer to early winter, but if you are growing from the same corms every year the earliest you can plant will, to some extent, be governed by the previous flowering time, as the corms should be given a resting period for the flowers to die off and the corms to ripen.

Corms can be left in the old compost in the pots until you are ready to plant, and when you separate them from the compost you should find that a substantial number of cormlets of different sizes have been produced. The largest ones will flower in the spring but the smaller ones will need a season's growth before becoming large enough to flower.

You will appreciate from this that freesias are very economical to grow, because once you have made your initial purchase your stock will grow each year and in three or four years you will have twice as many corms as you wish to grow.

It is necessary to repot freesias annually, in fresh compost to obtain the best results.

HIPPEASTRUM (FAMILY AMARYLLIDACEAE)

The bulbs usually offered are all hybrids and there are a number of named varieties such as 'Apple Blossom' (white with pink markings), 'Happy

Memory' (white with red markings), 'Fire Dance' (red), 'Excelsior' (orange) and 'Mont Blanc' (white). Usually, however, they are only offered under a colour description such as red or orange. In Great Britain the first hybrid was raised by Arthur Johnson in 1799 by crossing *Hippeastrum reginae* with *H. vittatum* and was named *Hippeastrum × johnsonii*.

There are several species which are worth growing should you develop a keen interest in these plants. *H.*

equestre, sometimes called the Barbados Lily, is a vivid scarlet with greenish markings at the base of the petals. It is of West Indian origin. *H. vittatum* is creamy white with red stripes, from Central Andes. *H. candidum* has drooping white blooms, and is fragrant and summer flowering, from Argentina. *H. aulicum* is a rich red with green at the base of the petals. It has much narrower petals, more like a sprekelia, and is winter flowering, It originates in Brazil.

Hippeastrums are usually grown from bulbs, which

Hippeastrum hybrids have very large showy flowers.

are readily available. They can be raised from seed but take about three years to reach flowering size, consequently it is hardly worthwhile to adopt this method of growing, unless a large number of plants is required.

Any good compost can be used, such as JI No.2, or a soilless compost. Select the pot according to the size of the bulb, the ideal being a pot which leaves a space of 1 in (2.5 cm) between the bulb and the side of the pot. Plant the bulb in the pot to leave about one third of the bulb above the level of the compost, which in turn should be about 1 in (2.5 cm) below the top of the pot. Water the compost by filling the pot with water up to the brim and then place the pot in the propagator at a temperature of 60−65°F (15−18°C).

A good time to pot the plants is late winter, and by the beginning of spring the flower buds should be showing. As soon as the whole of the flower bud has grown out of the bulb and you can see the stem, move the plant out of the propagator to a cooler temperature. At this stage a day temperature of 50−60°F (10−15°C) will ensure steady strong growth, and will produce a sturdy plant. If allowed to remain too long in the propagator, in a temperature of some 60−70°F (15−18°C), the stem and also the leaves would tend to make sappy weak growth. The plants will stand a minimum night temperature of 45°F (7°C) without suffering any harm.

You may have read that hippeastrums flower before the leaves grow, but this is not so with modern hybrids, and all the bulbs I have grown during the last ten years have always grown leaves before the flower bud has appeared.

The appearance of the plant is very much more attractive when it has well-formed leaves at the time of flowering, and bulbs which fail to produce leaves until after the bulb has flowered are not really worth a place in a grower's collection.

Sometimes it happens that a bulb will send up leaves and no flower bud appears. Should this happen, reduce the watering and keep the compost dry until the bud appears and then water normally.

After the bulb has flowered and the petals have withered allow the stem to remain for a few weeks, then cut it off at the point where it emerges from the bulb. Keep the plant watered until the middle of summer, with an occasional suitable feed, after which new leaves are not likely to form so the pot can be allowed to gradually dry out by the end of the summer. During late summer the object is to ripen the bulb, hence the plants should be put in the sunniest place in the greenhouse.

During the winter the bulbs are left in their pots in the dry compost, and can be kept under a bench in the greenhouse providing that a minimum temperature of 45°F (7°C) is usually maintained. An occasional drop to 40°F (5°C) on very cold nights will not harm the bulbs providing the compost is dust-dry and devoid of any moisture.

Hippeastrums should be repotted in fresh compost every year. It will be found that the increase in the size of the bulb, by the year's growth, sometimes necessitates potting on into a larger pot. If one is to expect a strong healthy plant the following season, it is only logical to do everything possible to encourage the growth of the bulb, and this is done by giving the plant the best possible environment and a suitable compost. Advice on the culture of hippeastrums often states that the bulb only needs repotting every three years, but during the second and third years there would be very little plant food available to the bulb. Moreover, the bulb grows in size, and in three years should be appreciably larger, consequently the pot would be too small during the third year. It is better to repot every year, and no useful purpose is served in leaving the bulb undisturbed for three years; in fact, quite the reverse is true.

HYACINTHUS (FAMILY LILIACEAE)

The Dutch hyacinth is one of the best known, and widely grown, spring bulbs; everyone with any interest in pot plants must have grown one at one time or another. The species was being grown in Europe as early as the sixteenth century, and found particular favour in the Netherlands, with the result that the Dutch became specialists in the growing and raising of new varieties, and a large nursery industry became established, which flourishes to this day.

The cultivation of Dutch hyacinths is comparatively simple, but there are one or two important points to watch if you wish to ensure that your efforts meet with success. The usual time to start the bulbs into growth is autumn for flowering sometime during the period mid-winter to early spring. You can buy Christmas-flowering hyacinths, which are bulbs that have been specially treated, and these should be potted in late summer.

It is important not to mix different colours, of

Hyacinthus 'Delft Blue'.

Hyacinthus 'Pink Pearl'.

which there is quite a wide range mostly in shades of reds and blues. When potting two or more bulbs together in the same bowl, make sure the bulbs are all the same variety and, if possible, all the same size. The purpose of this is to produce a bowl of hyacinth with flowers all in bloom at the same time.

You have a wide choice of composts, none of which is better than another, but if you wish to grow hyacinths in bowls without any drainage holes it is better to use either bulb fibre or a soilless compost. Alternatively you can grow the bulb in water, for which purpose special glass vases are made.

A good method to use for potting hyacinths is to put a layer of compost in the container, then place the bulbs on this, as far apart as the container will allow. Ensure that there is space between the bulbs and that they are not touching each other, then press compost down around the bulbs, leaving about ½ in (13 mm) of the tip of the bulb above the compost.

Give the compost a good watering and allow the surplus water to drain away. When planting in bowls, the way to do this is to hold the bowl at the steepest angle that the contents will allow without spilling out of the bowl; this causes the excess water to appear at the end of the bowl. When watering hyacinths in

104

bowls, which do not have any drainage holes, it is rather difficult to know whether you have overwatered, and you should use this method to check.

After potting and watering, the bulbs must be kept in complete darkness, in a cool atmosphere, for the next six to ten weeks. Where you will keep the bulbs will depend on your circumstances but it is essential that the containers are kept in a cool atmosphere because warmth at this stage could be detrimental. Should you not have any suitable accommodation your best procedure would be to bury the containers, under about 4 in (10 cm) of peat, in the garden.

Examine the plants every seven to ten days and water only if absolutely necessary. As soon as the shoots are about 1 to 2 in (2.5-5 cm) high the bulbs should be placed in a shady spot, ideally in an atmosphere of about 50°F (10°C). If you do not have a suitable spot available, make cardboard cones and place these over the growing stems for about ten days.

First of all the leaves will develop and then, as these grow, the flower bud will appear. At this stage the container should be moved to a warmer situation; about 60 – 70°F (15 – 21°C) is ideal. If the container is in the house, on a window-ledge, it should be turned regularly to ensure that all the shoots receive an equal amount of light; otherwise growth could be uneven and spoil the overall appearance. Keep the compost moist at all times.

After flowering cut off the flower heads, leaving the stems intact, continue watering and also feed the bulbs about once a fortnight with a general liquid feed. In due course the leaves will wither, and when this happens cease watering, allow the bulbs to dry, and store during the summer in a cool place if possible.

In the autumn the bulbs can be planted about 2 in (5 cm) deep in the garden. They can be left in the garden indefinitely and should bloom for many years.

As mentioned, hyacinths can be grown in water and, in this instance, it is usually a single bulb growing in a special type of glass vase, which is shaped to hold the bulb in a firm upright position. A bulb grown in water needs the same conditions as already described, the only difference being the medium in which it is being grown. The best water to use is rainwater. Fill the vase with water until the surface of the water is just below the bottom of the bulb and not touching it. As the roots grow the level of the water can be allowed to drop until it is about ½ – 1 in (13 – 25 mm) below the bottom of the bulb. It should be kept at this level by topping up, from time to time, if necessary. The water should not be changed throughout the whole cycle of the hyacinth's growth.

NERINE (FAMILY AMARYLLIDACEAE)

The nerine is a deciduous bulbous plant and the plants usually grown are derived from two species: *Nerine sarniensis* and *N. bowdenii.*

Nerine 'Blenheim'. This rarely seen pot plant has an ethereal beauty.

N. sarniensis is the species commonly known as the Guernsey lily. The name originated in the same way as the Scarborough lily. According to one version bulbs were washed ashore on the coast of Guernsey from a shipwreck and began to grow. When the local inhabitants saw the beautiful flowers they commenced cultivating them and the blooms were sent as cut flowers to the English markets.

Nerines are natives of South Africa and *N. sarniensis* is not frost-hardy and requires warmer conditions than *N. bowdenii* which is the hardiest of the species.

Nerines take three years to flower when grown from seed, so it is usual to purchase bulbs which should be potted in summer in an acid compost such as compost E2 with at least one third of the bulb above the soil level in 4-in or 4½-in (10 or 11-cm) pots depending on the size of the bulb. After potting water the plants and when growth commences water moderately during the growing season which is from summer to spring. Cease watering when the leaves begin to yellow or at the end of the spring and keep quite dry from spring to late summer. Place the bulbs

in full sunlight in the greenhouse to ripen. It is only necessary to repot every three or four years.

Nerine bowdenii has pink flowers and blooms early to mid-autumn. *N. sarniensis* ranges in colour from pale purple through red and pink to white. The original species is a glowing scarlet red. Sometimes it sends up a stem and flowers before the leaves appear and at other times the flower stem and leaves appear at the same time.

The nerine is a useful plant because it flowers in the autumn when not many flowering plants are available.

SPREKELIA (FAMILY AMARYLLIDACEAE)

From Mexico and Guatemala, *Sprekelia formosissima* was named in honour of Johann Heinrich Von Sprekelsen (1691 to 1764). It has an unusual flower, red in colour, and as it is very easy to grow it is well worth growing two or three bulbs as a variation from other bulbous plants. Sprekelias require exactly the same treatment as hippeastrums in all respects, and if started into growth at the same time will usually flower a few weeks later than a hippeastrum. Propagation is by offsets which form very freely.

Sprekelia formosissima, the Jacobean Lily, blooms in the spring.

VALLOTA (FAMILY AMARYLLIDACEAE)

Vallota speciosa, the Scarborough Lily, is a delightful bulbous plant.

The popular name in Britain for *Vallota speciosa* is the Scarborough lily, and according to legend it acquired this name because bulbs were washed ashore at Scarborough from a shipwreck, and the local inhabitants planted the bulbs, thus the plant became quite common in the town of Scarborough. It is native to South Africa.

Bulbs can be potted in late autumn or preferably in spring using JI No.2 or a soilless compost. The bulbs are rather small and a better effect is obtained if three bulbs are planted in a 4½-in (11.5-cm) pot rather than planting singly, in which latter case a 3½-in (9-cm) pot would suffice. After potting place the pots on the greenhouse bench in the heated part, where the average temperature is 45 – 50°F (7 – 10°C) during the autumn or the spring. Vallotas should not be forced into growth but allowed to grow naturally and they will stand a minimum winter temperature of 40°F (5°C).

If the bulbs are potted in spring they should be watered as required, and if you are very fortunate will flower in late summer, after which from early autumn until the following spring the plants should be watered sparingly and kept on the dry side to allow the bulbs to rest during the winter months. Repotting is only required every other year and is simply for the purpose of renewing the compost, which would contain very little nutrient after two years. Use the same size of pot.

Begonia rex hybrids are very colourful foliage plants which are available in a wide variety of leaf patterns and colours.

FOLIAGE PLANTS

During the winter months, it is very difficult to provide a sufficient number of flowering pot plants to meet your house requirements; so during this period foliage plants become essential. In this context it is to be understood that the term 'house plant' refers to plants which are grown for their foliage, the flowers of such plants, being very insignificant, are usually removed when they appear.

The ten house plants covered by this chapter are all plants which I have grown in the house over long periods of time, sometimes over three years in the same place, and they are all plants which will not just survive but will thrive in the usual conditions of centrally-heated houses.

BEGONIA REX (FAMILY BEGONIACEAE)

These plants are regarded by some gardeners as the most beautiful of all the foliage plants. They certainly exist in a very wide range of leaf patterns and colours and a large well-grown plant is a magnificent sight.

The species *Begonia rex* was a chance import into England in 1756 and its potentiality was quickly recognised by nurserymen with the result that it was propagated and also used for breeding. As a parent plant it has the remarkable property that no matter which species it is crossed with the resulting progeny always possesses the characteristics of the *rex* species. The plants sold today under the description *Begonia rex* are, of course, all varieties and not the original *Begonia rex* species, which is seldom seen nowadays.

The species has the typical begonia shape of leaf, but it is smooth-edged, of dark metallic olive green, with a silvery green band marking along the leaf, running parallel to the edges. It comes from Assam. Some of the best hybrids have been produced by crossing it with *Begonia diadema* which gave hybrids leaves with jagged edges, and *Begonia decora* which introduced a red coloration into the leaves. In the past, as with many other plants, there were numerous named varieties such as 'King Henry', 'Silver Queen', 'Helene Teupel' and 'Friede', but nowadays it is very difficult to obtain a named variety and it is merely a question of choosing a plant with leaf markings which appeal to you.

A suitable compost for *Begonia rex* is compost E6 or JI potting compost No.2. but it is perhaps easier to grow them in soilless compost, and my experience has been that they grow faster in this medium and are easier to maintain during the winter months.

The easiest way to propagate these plants is to select a young leaf which is growing vigorously in early summer and break it off, making sure that the whole of the stem is intact. Using a 4½-in (11.5-cm) half pot, about half filled with soilless cutting compost, insert the stems of the leaves about ½ in (13 mm) deep in the compost, after dipping the end of the stem in a hormone rooting powder. A pot this size is suitable for four leaf cuttings, and the whole should be enclosed inside a polythene bag secured by folding the open end underneath the pot. The cutting compost should be moist but free from excess water, otherwise it could cause the cuttings to rot when wholly enclosed in a polythene bag. Examine the cuttings from time to time because the close damp conditions sometimes cause a part of the leaf or even the whole cutting to rot, and if this is not removed it will spread to the other cuttings.

When the cuttings have grown roots they should be potted in the potting compost complete with the old leaf. The roots are produced at the base of the leaf stem and it usually takes several weeks before tiny new leaves develop. When these have grown about ½ in (13 mm) long, the old leaf can then be discarded by cutting the old stem as close to the new plant as possible.

The ideal conditions for growth are a place in a good light, but not direct sunlight, and a temperature of 60–70°F (15–21°C) in the summer when the plants should be growing strongly. Old plants tend to have a resting period in the winter and only grow very slowly, but young plants grown from cuttings taken earlier in the year will grow quite vigorously if kept in a humid atmosphere at 55–60°F (13–15°C).

Plants benefit very considerably by being potted on in larger pots when ready, and this is usually quite apparent as the plant will begin to look too large for the pot.

Plants growing in the house must be carefully watered, particularly in the winter, to ensure they are not overwatered. Wait until the surface of the compost is dry to the touch and test the weight of the plant as a double check before giving the plant water.

CALATHEA (FAMILY MARANTACEAE)

Known in the United States of America as the 'peacock plant' it has beautiful glossy leaves usually about 6 in (15 cm) long, but sometimes they become elongated and grow to two or three times longer. The upper side of the leaf has an attractive dark green marking on a silvery green background with a light green edging. On the underside of the leaf the pattern of the dark green marking appears in a maroon colour.

Calatheas originate in Brazil and they require exactly the same treatment as marantas. The method of propagation is also the same.

HEDERA (FAMILY ARALIACEAE)

The members of this genus are all climbers and are very widely used as house plants. *Hedera* is the latin for ivy, and although there are seven species in the genus it is the varieties raised from *Hedera helix* and *H. canariensis* which are so popular as house plants.

H.C. foliis variegatis is better known, and invariably referred to, as Canary Island ivy, and it does indeed come from the Canary Islands, as well as Madeira and the Azores. It is a cultivar with very attractive leaves which have green centres and pale cream edges. The leaves are interesting in that no two leaves are identical. These plants are completely tolerant to

Hedera canariensis or Canary Island Ivy is a useful and easy-to-grow climbing or trailing plant.

Hedera helix 'Goldchild', with its attractive leaves, is a good plant for the porch as it will tolerate cold conditions.

house conditions and will survive considerable neglect, which makes them ideal house plants.

A soilless compost is ideal as they prefer an open compost with plenty of fibre and ideally slightly acid (pH 5.5 to 6). The best way to grow an attractive display is to put three or four plants in a 3½-in (9-cm) pot and either grow the plants climbing upwards on a suitable support, or allow the growth to trail downwards when positioned, say, on a plant stand. They are slow growers and resent being overpotted consequently should be left in the same pot for as long as three or four years and the final potting in a 5-in (13-cm) pot.

As with most house plants it is better to underwater than to overwater, and if leaves turn yellow and drop it will usually indicate the plant is being over watered.

This variety of ivy is not self-branching and an annual stopping, by removing the growing tip, usually causes more vigorous growth.

LILY FAMILY (LILIACEAE)

This large family contains some of the best house plants, which are so varied in appearance that it is difficult to believe that they are members of the same family. The family includes 220 genera and over 3,500 species, many of which are familiar names to everyone, such as tulips, hyacinths, lilies, asparagus, aspidistras and so on.

We are only concerned with four genera, all of which are very easy to grow, which is a characteristic of numerous members of this family. These four genera are all quite different in appearance and consequently offer considerable variety. Firstly we have *Chlorophytum*, which has long thin leaves similar to grass, followed by *Cordyline* which has broad coloured leaves growing from a single stem, then *Sanseveria*, which has thick sword-like fleshy leaves growing upright from soil level, and, finally, *Dracaena deremensis* which has long pointed glossy leaves growing out spirally from a thick single stem.

Chlorophytum comosum 'Variegatum', the Spider Plant.

CHLOROPHYTUM COMOSUM

First introduced in 1751 this plant comes from South Africa. It is commonly known as the spider plant, due to its habit of producing very long thin stems which grow from the centre of the plant; at the end of these stems plantlets form, and if these rest on the surface of a growing medium roots quickly form at the base of the plantlet.

To propagate *C. comosum* all one has to do is to fill a 2½ or 3-in (6 or 7.5-cm) pot with compost and pin the plantlet to the surface. A simple method is to use a hairpin or a short piece of wire bent into the shape of a hairpin. After a few weeks the plants will have rooted and the stem joining it to the parent plant is then severed.

The plants offered for sale are all the 'Variegatum' forms which have a white stripe running along the centre of the leaves.

Chlorophytums are possibly the easiest house plants of all to grow. Any ordinary potting compost or soilless compost will suffice. They will tolerate sunshine or shade, warm or cold conditions, dry or moist air, and any amount of neglect.

Fig.10 Chlorophytums can easily be propagated by means of the small plantlets which form at the tips of long arching stems produced during active growth. After dipping the base of the plantlet in hormone rooting powder, ensure that it is kept in close contact with the compost, in small pots, by means of a hairpin or bent wire.

However, as with all plants, we should endeavour to provide the most suitable growing conditions and for this plant the best conditions are a good light, watering only when the compost has dried on the surface and potting on when necessary, usually discarding plants when they are too big for a 6-in (15-cm) pot.

CORDYLINE TERMINALIS

This plant is sometimes offered for sale as *Dracaena terminalis*, but do not let this confuse you as they are one and the same plant. The species has plain green leaves but many cultivars have been raised and there are numerous named varieties, but as with *Begonia rex*, nowadays the plants are offered unnamed and you merely select the leaf colouring which appeals to you. They are often somewhat expensive because young plants do not develop coloured leaves, consequently the plants have to be grown on for some years by the nurserymen before being offered for sale.

Cordylines are very tolerant plants and grow very well in a soilless compost given the same treatment as chlorophytums.

Cordyline terminalis. The colouring of the leaves gives this plant its attraction.

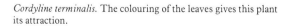

DRACAENA DEREMENSIS

The variety 'Bausei' has been raised from the species, which is a native of Derema in the Usambara region of East Africa. It is a very elegant plant with glossy dark green leaves with two white stripes along the length of the leaf, in between which there is a greyish-green band. Once you have acquired this plant and sited it in a suitable place you have a permanent resident in your home which will grow taller and more elegant each year. The one I have is about five years old and is almost 3 ft (1 m) tall. It has been standing in the same position at the back of the living room for the last three years and gets most of its light, particularly in the winter, from a pair of wall lights. Without this artificial light I do not think it would have thrived as it has, because originally it was in a poor light and lost one or two of its lower leaves.

It will grow satisfactorily in a soilless compost and is not a demanding plant other than requiring a warm temperature, being definitely a plant for the living room. As with the other plants in this group it is very tolerant of underwatering and is consequently better if watered only when the compost surface is completely dry.

Dracaena deremensis a very good house plant and with care will last for years.

SANSEVIERIA TRIFASCIATA

This plant was named after a nobleman Raimondo de Sango, Prince of Sanseviero, who lived in the eighteenth century. Being a rather difficult name to pronounce it is commonly known as 'mother-in-law's tongue'. The most attractive cultivar to grow is *S. trifasciata* 'Laurentii' in which the leaves are edged by golden yellow bands.

Sansevierias have stiff tough bayonet-like leaves which are dark green with patterns of grey or silvery green markings and additionally in the case of the variety 'Laurentii', yellow bands at the leaf edges. They grow from rhizomes and will throw up side shoots which when several inches high can be severed complete with roots from the parent plant. When

Sanseviera zeylanica is often known as Mother-in-law's Tongue.

new plants are raised by this method the yellow band is retained, but if new plants are raised by leaf cuttings the yellow marking is lost. The method of taking cuttings is to cut a mature leaf into sections 2–4 in (5–10 cm) long, allow the cut surface to dry and then insert one end in a cutting compost. Keep in a minimum temperature of 70°F (21°C). Roots take at least a month to form.

It is a slow growing plant and a more pleasing effect is obtained by potting three plants to a pot using compost E6 or JI No.2. Plants do not need repotting for years, and then only when they look too large for the pot.

Like most plants with fleshy leaves, sansevieras will withstand long periods of drought and will not die by being underwatered. On the other hand overwatering can prove fatal. They are very tolerant plants and will grow in sun or shade and cool or warm conditions.

MARANTA LEUCONEURA VAR. KERCHOVEANA (FAMILY MARANTACEAE)

There are some 26 genera and 280 species in the Marantaceae family and many of them make excellent house plants. Marantas were named after a sixteenth-century botanist Bartolomes Maranti and their native habitat is the rain forests of Brazil. The popular name for *M. leuconeura* 'Kerchoveana' is the 'prayer plant', because of the way its leaves move in the dark. When the plant is exposed to full daylight its leaves lie quite flat in a horizontal position but at night when the plant is in the dark the leaves stand up vertically, often in pairs, as if in prayer.

Marantas are warm house plants and do best in temperatures of 65–70°F (18–21°C) by day with minimum night temperatures of 60°F (15°C). They like a good growing medium such as compost E6 and a good light but shading from sunlight.

When the prayer plant is happy with its environment and consequently growing well it produces small insignificant white flowers. Water sparingly particularly in the winter and always allowing the top compost to dry out.

Propagation is by division of the roots and can be carried out at any time. As the plant grows it will fill the pot with roots, and a 4½-in (11.5-cm) pot should be regarded as the final potting size, unless for some reason you wish to grow a large plant.

With a plant of this type, taking into account the size of the leaves, you lose something in form by growing too large a plant in a large pot.

Repotting can be done at any time of the year so when you think it is necessary, knock the plant out of the pot and divide it into two or three parts depending on the size of plant you are splitting.

You will observe that the maranta makes its growth by sending up new shoots from the roots and it is very easy to separate the different shoots complete with roots.

Maranta leuconera 'Kerchoveana', the Prayer Plant, is easy to grow in the house.

116

TRADESCANTIA AND ZEBRINA (FAMILY COMMELINACEAE)

Tradescantias were named after John Tradescant who lived in the seventeenth century and was perhaps the most famous gardener in England at that time.

Tradescantia fluminensis is a very useful trailing plant for hanging baskets or plant stands.

Tradescantia fluminensis 'Variegata' is the cultivar most often grown, and it is sometimes referred to as the 'wandering Jew'. It is a very useful trailing plant for hanging baskets and plant stands. It will grow in any kind of compost, as it is a most adaptable plant, and cuttings, taken at a leaf joint on the stem, will root with such ease at any time of the year that you cannot fail to have a replacement plant available whenever it may be required. It is a very good plant for the interior of rooms as it will grow very successfully in a poor light.

Zebrina pendula is very similar in both habit and culture requirements to tradescantia, from which it differs mainly in the colouring of the leaves. Tradescantias have green leaves with longitudinal white stripes varying in width, whereas *Zebrina pendula* has a central dark green longitudinal central stripe on a silvery green leaf with dark green edges. Depending on the conditions of growth the central stripe, which is quite broad, can change to purple; when this happens the green margins also change to purple. The underside of the leaves is always a deep maroon colour. To develop the purple coloration, plants need to be grown in warm conditions in a reasonably good light.

Zebrina pendula 'Quadricolour' is a very colourful trailing plant.

117

Agapanthus africanus 'Diana'.

EXOTIC PLANTS

One of the advantages of having a greenhouse is that it enables you to grow any plant which appeals to you, regardless of its cultural requirements, and in the course of trying out different plants over the years for their suitability as house plants, I have occasionally come across a plant which has given me considerable pleasure.

The four plants included in this section are worth a place in the greenhouse, and, as they are perennials, once they have been acquired they become a permanent part of the collection.

One would not wish to grow more than two or three plants of each, but I would always wish to grow at least one because they all have their own special appeal for me and give me great pleasure each year as they bloom.

AGAPANTHUS (FAMILY LILIACEAE)

Agapanthus africanus, sometimes known as the African lily, is a cool greenhouse perennial with a fleshy tuberous root. It was introduced from Cape Province, South Africa, to Europe in the seventeenth century. It is of compact habit, with graceful strap-shaped leaves similar to a hippeastrum. From these a stem grows to a height of some 18−30 in (45−75 cm), bearing a large round flower head or umbel made up of pale blue tubular florets. There is also a white variety.

Pot the tuberous root about 6 in (15 cm) deep in a 7-in (17.5-cm) pot in compost E6 or JI No.2 in early spring. Water the pot and until growth appears water sparingly, after which put the pot on the automatic watering bench until the end of spring, then put the plant outside in a sunny position. If the plant is left in the greenhouse during the summer it is likely that the flowering stem will become elongated. Although these plants will stand full sunshine, they do not require a hot atmosphere. The blooming period is usually during summer. Cease watering at the end of the summer and keep the compost completely dry from autumn until the following spring when the plant can be started into growth merely by watering it. No artificial heat is required as the normal unheated greenhouse temperatures at this time of the year are quite high enough during the day to bring the plant into growth. Agapanthus are quite hardy and only require a frost-proof storage in the winter months when dormant. Repot plants every three or four years, at which time you can increase your stock by root division.

BRUNFELSIA (FAMILY SOLANACEAE)

In California where it grows outdoors, *Brunfelsia calycina* is called 'Yesterday, Today and Tomorrow', due to the changing colour of its flower. It opens purple, becomes lavender and gradually fades to almost white. In a hot climate this colour change can take place in three days, but in the greenhouse in cooler parts it takes much longer.

It is a small evergreen shrub native to the West Indies and Brazil, very slow-growing, and it is difficult to get it to bush as it does not readily produce side shoots. Plants should be repotted in the spring when necessary about every two or three years using compost E6.

Remove all the compost from the roots and repot in the same pot unless the plant obviously requires a larger size. Even after seven or eight years it is not likely to require larger than a 5-in (12.5-cm) pot.

Brunfelsias like a warm moist atmosphere and bright light. Given ideal conditions they will flower continuously from early summer to late autumn, but as they are not likely to get ideal conditions when growing in a greenhouse with many other plants they usually have a burst of flowering in early summer and then flower spasmodically throughout the rest of the season.

During the growing season ample water should be provided, but by mid-autumn watering should cease until the compost is fairly dry, and only sufficient water should be given in the winter months to prevent the compost from drying out completely. If

Brunfelsia calycina has unusual flowers which change colour from purple to pale lavender.

the plant is treated in this manner it will stand night temperatures as low as 40°F (4°C). Ideally a minimum winter temperature of 50°F (10°C) is recommended, and in a severe winter when day and night temperatures are very low for prolonged periods it might cause the brunfelsia to lose one or two leaves; but if the compost is dry it will not suffer any ill effects at a minimum temperature of 40°F (4°C).

Propagation is carried out in the spring, selecting a half-ripened shoot 2–3 in (5–7.5 cm) and using a soilless rooting compost. When the cutting is about 6 in (15 cm) tall, it should be pinched out. Mature plants should also have their growing tips pinched out in the spring every year, otherwise the plant will tend to grow straggly.

CLIVIA (FAMILY AMARYLLIDACEAE)

Clivia miniata is a greenhouse evergreen which was first introduced to Great Britain in 1823 from South Africa. Formerly it was called *Imantophyllum*, but in around 1866, when a new classification was introduced, it was re-named *Clivia*, after Charlotte, Duchess of Northumberland, née Clive, who is said to have been the first to flower the plant in England. It has the common names Kaffir or Caffre lily and Natal lily, which no doubt were used when it bore its former name, but the use of these has died out now that it has such a simple generic name.

It has very fleshy roots and strap-like leaves of which when it is growing well, it will produce four to six new ones during the growing season. It flowers in the spring.

Clivias are not difficult to raise from seed, and once you have a plant propagation of further plants can be carrried out by means of offshoots, which frequently form on flowering size plants. The only drawback to raising your plants from seed is that you will have to wait three or four years before you see it flower. On the other hand flowering-size plants are expensive. In my ignorance of the length of time it takes the plant to flower, I bought a packet of seeds in 1956 for three shillings. It contained three seeds which I sowed on 9 April 1956, and all three germinated. It was four years before the first plant flowered, but the tremendous pleasure it gave me was worth all the time I had waited. I still have three clivias which have been propagated from time to time from these original plants. It is necessary to discard plants after a number of years, because they would require very large pots or tubs and take up too much room in the greenhouse.

Clivias are not demanding plants and require very little attention. Having raised a young plant from seed it should be kept growing steadily throughout the year. A minimum temperature of 45°F (7°C) in the winter will suffice.

During the winter months growth will be very slow and little watering will be required. As the plant grows in size, it should be repotted only when the fleshy roots fill the pot using compost E6 or JI No.3. A 6 or 7-in (15 or 17.5-cm) pot will be required by the time the plant has reached flowering size, but do not overpot because plants are most likely to bloom when they are pot-bound.

The treatment of mature plants is quite different in so far as the plant is rested from mid-autumn until late winter by withholding water. Commence watering again in late winter, and if it is possible to give the plant warmer conditions, say 50-55°F (10–12°C), at this time it is beneficial, and flowering is more likely to occur. During the resting period clivias only need to be kept frost-free, but when started into growth they need a minimum night temperature of 45°F (7°C) if they are to make any growth.

When the clivia has flowered in spring it should begin to make new leaf growth. It is at this stage that feeding should take place, as well as potting on into a larger pot if required. Clivias which have reached

---

Clivia miniata is an elegant plant which flowers in the spring.

flowering size do not necessarily flower every year because it is not always possible to provide the ideal conditions.

If weather conditions during the winter are abnormally cold during the day as well as at night it is naturally impossible for the amateur grower to provide sufficient heat to meet the plant's minimum growth requirements. When temperatures are too low during the bud formation period it can result in a short flower stem with the flower remaining down in the leaves.

The plants grown today are not the species *Clivia miniata*, but varieties or hybrids which have been raised from the species. They are superior to the parent species, and although there are numerous varieties the most common is an orange-coloured flower.

HIBISCUS (FAMILY MALVACEAE)

The evergreen shrub *Hibiscus rosa-sinensis* has become one of the most popular plants for the house, which is not surprising because it produces most attractive flowers over a long period. It is said to have been discovered in southern China early in the eighteenth century, and it was introduced to Europe in 1731.

In warm climates where it is grown as an outdoor shrub it grows some 10–15 ft (3–4.5 m), but when pot-grown in the greenhouse young plants are usually about 1–2 ft (30–60 cm).

It will grow bushy naturally, but should you obtain a plant which is not it will soon respond to pruning of the upper shoots. Older plants should be cut back quite severely in late winter to encourage new growth. The plants have shiny green leaves, and although it is an evergreen it is liable to shed one or two leaves during the winter, particularly if the temperature falls much below 50°F (10°C) (which is the minimum winter temperature recommended).

Actually they will survive when kept in a greenhouse with a minimum temperature of 45°F (7°C) falling to 40°F (4°C) during very cold nights, but they will lose all their leaves and take many months to recover.

Compost E6 or JI No.2 is suitable for hibiscus plants as they are quite vigorous growers, when enjoying favourable conditions. They need good light, but should be lightly shaded from direct sunlight, and a warm temperature. Care should be taken not to overwater as this could cause root rot. Hibiscus can be grown very satisfactorily on self-watering trays.

Propagation is by cuttings off the shoots, in autumn or spring, and whether you select cuttings of ripe wood or young green growth you will have to be patient as they take quite some time to root, and you may experience some failures. The plants offered for sale are all varieties or hybrids raised from the species. There are many named varieties, but usually tthe plants are just offered un-named in different colours, ranging from red, pinks and orange shades to bright yellow, in single, semi-double and double flowers.

Hibiscus rosa sinensis, Rose of China. A shrubby plant with very attractive flowers.

Primula kewensis has fragrant yellow flowers.

INDEX

Numbers in bold refer to page numbers of colour illustrations; those in italics to line drawings.

PICTURE CREDITS

The publishers would like to thank the following for permission to reproduce colour illustrations.

Gordon Procter: pp. 8, 33, 35, 42–3, 52, 55, 61, 63, 64, 72, 74, 75, 76 (top and bottom), 88, 90–1, 92, 108, 116, 117 (top), 123.

Peter McHoy: pp. 15, 16, 32, 45, 46, 47, 48, 49, 50, 51, 54, 57, 65, 66, 67, 71, 80, 81, 82, 86, 87, 89, 94, 97, 98, 104 (top and bottom), 110, 112, 113, 114, 120–1, 122.

The Iris Hardwick Library of Photographs: pp. 34, 38.

Harry Smith Horticultural Photographic Collection: pp. 36–7, 68–9, 85, 111.

A-Z Botanical Collection: pp. 44, 96, 99, 100, 105, 106, 115.

Bernard Alfieri: title page, pp. 4–5, 58–9, 102, 107, 117, (bottom), 118.

Line drawings by Anita Lawrence.